International Economic Relations since 1945

> Schenk provides a superb introduction to the history of the most important international linkages that shape the global economy. The book ranges deftly over more than 100 years of economic history shedding light on how we got here from there. This is a crucial account for anyone seeking to understand the global economy today and where we may be headed in the near future.
>
> Christopher M. Meissner, *University of California, USA*

The international economy since 1945 has endured dramatic changes in its balance of power, from the early period of prosperity for industrialised nations to the 2008–9 global crisis. In this volume Catherine R. Schenk outlines these huge changes, examines how the world's economic leaders have tried to organise and influence the international economy and presents the key frameworks in which international economic relations have developed.

Focusing on the pattern of international trade, international investment and the changing organisation of the international monetary system, this volume takes a chronological approach of key time-frames, and shows how policy has impacted on the balance of the international economy. Major events such as European integration in the 1960s, the collapse of the international monetary system and oil crisis in the 1970s, the return of China to the international economy in the 1980s and emerging market crises in the 1990s are discussed within the context of key themes, including global economic and regulatory co-ordination, the role of American economic hegemony, the evolution of exchange rate policy and unequal development.

International Economic Relations since 1945 is the perfect guide for all students of economic history and international history, and for those seeking to understand recent economic trends through a longer term perspective.

Catherine R. Schenk is Professor of International Economic History at the University of Glasgow, UK. She is an Academician of the Academy of Social Sciences and a Fellow of the Royal Historical Society. Her publications include *Britain and the Sterling Area: From Devaluation to Convertibility in the 1950s* (Routledge, 1994), *Hong Kong as an International Financial Centre: Emergence and Development, 1945–1965* (Routledge, 2001), *Hong Kong SAR's Monetary and Exchange Rate Challenges: Historical Perspectives* (2008) and *The Decline of Sterling: Managing the Retreat of an International Currency 1945–1992* (2010).

The Making of the Contemporary World
Edited by Eric J. Evans and Ruth Henig

The Making of the Contemporary World series provides challenging interpretations of contemporary issues and debates within strongly defined historical frameworks. The range of the series is global, with each volume drawing together material from a range of disciplines – including economics, politics and sociology. The books in this series present compact, indispensable introductions for students studying the modern world.

International Economic Relations since 1945

Catherine R. Schenk

Routledge
Taylor & Francis Group

LONDON AND NEW YORK

First published 2011 by Routledge
2 Park Square, Milton Park, Abingdon, Oxon OX14 4RN

Simultaneously published in the USA and Canada
by Routledge
711 Third Avenue, New York, NY 10017

*Routledge is an imprint of the Taylor & Francis Group,
an informa business*

Typeset in Times New Roman by
Florence Production Ltd, Stoodleigh, Devon
Printed and bound in Great Britain by
TJ International Ltd, Padstow, Cornwall

British Library Cataloguing in Publication Data
A catalogue record for this book is available from the British Library

Library of Congress Cataloging-in-Publication Data
Schenk, Catherine R. (Catherine Ruth), 1964–
    International economic relations since 1945/Catherine R. Schenk. – 1st ed.
        p.cm. – (The making of the contemporary world)
        Includes index.
    1. International economic relations – History – 20th century.
    2. Monetary policy. 3. Economic development. 4. World politics.
    5. Financial crises. I. Title.
    HF1359.S342011
    337–dc22   2010048564

ISBN: 978–0–415–57076–3 (hbk)
ISBN: 978–0–415–57078–7 (pbk)
ISBN: 978–0–203–81726–1 (ebk)

For Duncan and Margaret and Archie

Contents

Figures

Tables

1 Introduction and overview

The international economy is essentially composed of flows of people, goods, capital and ideas. These four categories correspond to the main factors in the production of economic wealth, so the global distribution of these elements is clearly vital for how national economies perform. The most basic link between national and international economic performance is through the trade of goods and services. Until the eighteenth century it was believed that national accounts operated rather like household accounts; which is to say that the greater the surplus a country could earn through its sale of production the better. Selling more goods to foreigners than was bought from foreign states ensured the accumulation of reserves of gold that were vital for the conduct of war, which was the main preoccupation of most state rulers. From the eighteenth century, however, understanding of the gains from international trade was promoted through the writings of Adam Smith and, later, David Ricardo and others. They described how if each country or region specialised in producing those goods and services in which they were most productive and efficient, they could then sell surplus production to buy what the country was less efficient in producing. If each country took this approach of international specialisation of production, then the world's resources would be used as efficiently as possible within and between each nation. Through the more efficient use of resources, international trade allowed the best prospects for growth overall.

Intuitively, this principle of the gains from trade is as easy to understand as the seventeenth-century mercantilist quest for ever greater surpluses. At an individual level, with well developed markets we specialise in what we are best at doing and then sell the goods and services that we produce for cash to buy what we want but are less able to make well. By not having to grow our own food, raise our own sheep to make our own clothing and build our own homes, we achieve higher standards of living than we would through individual independent subsistence. So it is that countries that do not engage in any international trade subsist at a relatively low standard of living (one of the only remaining examples is North Korea). Of course, the gains from trade require markets that bring buyers and sellers together and finance to bridge the lag between production and consumption to allow goods to travel over time and distance. The character and efficiency of these markets and the speed and ease of flows of goods, people, money and ideas determine how much international specialisation can occur and how much (and who) will gain from international trade.

It is clear that not all individuals benefit equally from the exchange. When Wal-Mart increases imports of Chinese clothing produced by low-wage workers in a factory in Shenzhen and sells these products in their stores in the US, American consumers will tend to buy less of their own (more expensive) domestically produced clothing. The result may be fewer jobs for some Americans in the US clothing industry, but this international trade will increase the disposable income of a much broader range of American consumers, who now have access to cheaper clothing and can spend more of their money on other goods and services. Such distributional effects of international trade on different groups of people have attracted policy-makers to interfere in international economic relations to try to maximise the benefits and minimise the losses. Government-imposed barriers to trade include quotas (limits on the number of an item that can be imported) and tariffs (a tax on each item imported across the border). Each form of trade barrier raises the domestic price of foreign goods either by contracting supply, in the case of quotas, or increasing costs for importers who then pass these costs on to the final consumer, in the case of tariffs. The welfare effects of tariffs and quotas differ since the government gains revenue from a tariff and can spend that income to compensate consumers for higher prices while still protecting domestic producers. In the case of quotas, however, the benefits of higher prices go to the company or individual who has been granted the license to import a quantity of foreign goods, so there is a net welfare loss to the population. Quotas may also lead to corruption as individuals lobby the government or offer bribes to gain import licenses. These distributional effects mean that in the post-war years quotas have been considered a worse barrier to trade than tariffs.

The benefits of buying from the cheapest producer and selling wherever the product commands the highest price might be extended to the other elements of international economic relations. Thus, the ability of people to migrate across borders will allow labour to flow where it attracts the highest wages or the best standard of living. In the nineteenth century, the redis-tribution of labour from relatively crowded and poor European countrysides and cities to economies with greater natural resources and higher per capita income such as the United States, Canada, Australia and Brazil was one of the defining characteristics of the economic growth and globalisation of this era. This movement of people was greatly assisted by advances in transport technology – such as steam shipping and railways – that made long journeys quicker and less risky. The people brought their skills and savings with them as well as their ideas and creativity to contribute to economic growth in their new homelands. These farmers and labourers produced food and raw materials that could be exported to Europe in return for imports of manufactures, thus linking international migration with international trade and rising real incomes. From the early twentieth century, however, fears about the depressing effect of immigrants on the wages of existing local populations led to restrictions on international migration. As with movement of goods, flows of people also induce effects that are felt unequally among the population and make this exchange a source of contention.

The international exchange of ideas such as the communication of opportunities, the spread of innovation and other information flows over long distances also contributed to economic growth. As well as being embedded in the human capital of migrants, in the nineteenth century this flow of ideas and information was enhanced by technological advances such as the telegraph, which helped collapse the psychic distance of international economic relations by reducing the risk and time-lag for exchange. In the later twentieth century, information technology based on a much wider and extensive infrastructure of fibre-optic cables and satellite transmission was a driving feature of renewed social, cultural as well as economic globalisation.

The final element in our list of international economic relations is the flow of capital. Allowing international capital to flow to where it attracts the highest return is a vital element in the promotion of global economic prosperity. Capital might take the form of portfolio investment – such as the millions of pounds invested by middle class British savers in Canadian railway bonds in the nineteenth century. This international investment integrated the markets of vast resource-rich territories and enabled them to supply raw materials and wheat to the industrial heartlands of Europe. Capital flows might also take the form of foreign direct investment (FDI) by a company that establishes an office or factory to produce or distribute overseas. This was an important feature of nineteenth-century globalisation, but became even more prominent in the post-1945 decades as innovation in communication technologies and faster transport made it easier for companies to expand their activities. With the development of global supply chains shipping parts for assembly and finished products to final markets, foreign investment became closely linked to international trade patterns.

Developed in the 1960s, Raymond Vernon's product-cycle theory of global production posited that goods invented in countries with high levels of human capital would initially be produced in these advanced economies in small numbers at high cost and high price.[1] As international demand for the product increased in other wealthy economies, production would move to these high income economies to replace imports. As a product was further standardised, its production became more mechanised and less skilled, so the location of production would move to where labour costs were cheaper. This idea helps to explain the global spread of manufacturing for twentieth-century products such as televisions, semi-conductors and computers, where production originated in the US, moved to Europe and Japan in the middle of the century, and was mainly located in emerging economies by the end of the century.

In order to record flows of international exchange, governments collect this information in accounts known as the balance of payments. These accounts measure all the flows of funds across the border in each direction and the overall balance therefore comprises the net flow of funds in and out of the country. In its simplest form, the balance of payments is divided into three sections, including the current account, the capital account and balancing movements in foreign exchange reserves. The current account measures net trade in goods and services, net flows of migrants' remittances, net interest and profits earned on overseas investment and tourism. The capital account measures net flows of short-term and long-term investment, including foreign direct investment. A surplus in the current account, for example, might be balanced by a net outflow on the capital account. Any leftover overall surplus or deficit must be accommodated through accumulations or sales of foreign exchange reserves held at the central bank. The three accounts in the simple balance of payments must always balance since the net money spent on international economic transactions must have been generated somehow, either by earnings or other inflows from abroad or sales of reserves. The accounts are related in many ways; for example, foreign

Table 1.1 The balance of payments

Current account	Balance of trade in goods
	Net flows of interest, profits and dividends
	Net flows of tourism, royalty payments and other trade in services
Capital account	Net long-term investment
	Net short-term investment (including sales of government debt to foreign holders)
	Net foreign direct investment
Foreign exchange reserves	Net sales and purchases of foreign exchange by central monetary authority

direct investment by a company setting up a factory overseas will appear as an outward flow in the capital account and may generate exports of equipment and machinery, imports of final production back to the home country, and repatriated profits, which all appear in the current account.

This section has introduced the key international economic relations with which this book is concerned, and has also suggested that the distributional effects of international exchange have prompted policy-makers to interfere with this process. The next section provides an overview of the organisation of the international economy as states sought to maximise the benefits of international trade and payments.

The organisation of the international economy

The way that the international economy was organised in the 'long' twentieth century from about 1880 to the present can be understood as a sequence of policy choices in reaction to the Mundell-Fleming Trilemma.[2] The Trilemma posits that there are three opposing goals for policy-makers in governments and central banks: stable exchange rates, open capital markets, sovereignty over domestic monetary policy. In the somewhat stylised world of economics, only two out of these three options are possible at any one time for relatively small, open economies. The largest economy at the anchor of the system will be the only one that can pursue policy autonomy in a context of free capital flows and fixed exchange rates. We can think of it using the following example. If a country sets a fixed value for its currency in terms of an anchor currency (sterling in the early part of the century or the US dollar after 1955) then it must follow the interest rate policy of the anchor. Otherwise, if interest rates rise abroad, for example, capital will flow out to get the higher returns overseas, demand for foreign currency will rise in the foreign exchange market and demand for domestic currency will fall so that there is pressure for the market rate to fall. A central bank might be able to protect the market price of its currency (the exchange rate) for a while by selling foreign currency and buying up domestic currency, but eventually the central bank will run out of reserves. To stop this happening and still retain the pegged exchange rate, either domestic interest rates must rise to stem the outflow, or residents must be prevented from buying foreign investments or currency. To have a pegged exchange rate either the government gives up its ability to set its own interest rate or imposes controls on international flows of capital. If it abandons the peg and allows the market to determine the exchange rate, then capital can flow freely and the central bank can set whatever interest rate it likes. In practice, of course, very few countries completely ignore their exchange rate in determining their economic policy since fluctuations can have a real impact on domestic incomes by changing the price of imports and exports (that is, currency appreciation makes foreign currency and foreign goods cheaper in terms of domestic currency and vice versa for depreciation). The trilemma is only a stylised tool of analysis, and compromises among the choices can also be found, such as limiting convertibility and free capital flows to a smaller group of countries or trading bloc in order to retain some degree of policy independence from a large economy outside the bloc – as happened with the inter-war Sterling Bloc. Nevertheless, the trilemma provides a useful framework in which to understand the evolution of international economic relations and the choices available to policy-makers.

Under the classic gold standard from about 1880, a fixed exchange rate system based on a defined value of each currency in terms of gold operated relatively smoothly with open international capital markets only because of the willingness of national governments to conform their interest rate policies to global levels led by the Bank of England. There were some currency and financial crises on the margins of the system, such as in South America, but for the most part the system functioned well and was associated with an era of globalised markets in labour, capital and trade and sustained economic growth, particularly for emerging market economies, such as Canada, the United States and Australia. After the disruptions of the First World War, the effort to restore this system foundered on the unwillingness of states to sacrifice their policy sovereignty in favour of stable exchange rates. For Britain in particular, the restraint on domestic economic policy required to sustain an overvalued sterling–US dollar exchange rate proved costly to economic prosperity through the later 1920s. In retrospect, the

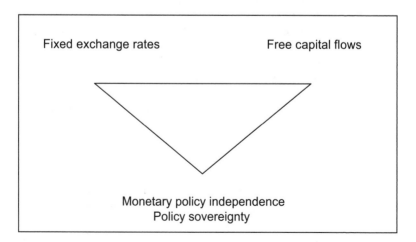

Figure 1.1 Policy trilemma

inability to pursue expansionary policies that might have mitigated the pain of the Great Depression was blamed on invidious free capital flows that allowed speculators to undermine national monetary policies given the pegged exchange rate regime. From 1929, the collapse of the US economy dragged other countries down into worsened recession as they sought to restrain capital outflow attracted by higher US interest rates as the American monetary system contracted. Eichengreen has convincingly argued that it was only by abandoning their pegged exchange rates that economies were able to pursue the expansionary policies that pulled them out of the Great Depression.[3] He describes the pegged rate system of the inter-war period as 'golden fetters' that constrained economic policy in the context of relatively open capital markets. As described in Chapter 2, this experience is fundamental to how policy-makers approached the design of the post-war international economy.

The post-war solution to the trilemma sought to restore policy sovereignty to national governments while retaining the perceived benefits of stable, pegged exchange rates. With broad commitments in many countries to welfare spending, full employment and prosperity for their populations, the governments of developed states in particular had adopted much greater responsibility for national economic management than their predecessors. Their two priorities (policy sovereignty and stable exchange rates) required tight controls against speculative and short-term capital flows that could disrupt the pegged exchange rates if interest rates diverged between states. As currencies became more easily exchanged for trading purposes from the end of the 1950s, however, it became more and more difficult to control speculative movements of capital. Financial innovation by banks to offer more services for their increasingly international customers in the 1960s added to the ease of evading national regulations on international financial flows. In particular, the development of so-called 'offshore' financial markets outside national supervision and control grew quickly during this decade. These developments all undermined the ability of national governments to continue to retain pegged exchange rates while pursuing independent interest rate policies. Periodically the market lost confidence in the ability and commitment of governments to defend their exchange rates and pushed a currency off from its peg either through a revaluation (as in the case of the Deutschmark) or devaluation (as in the case of sterling or the franc), making substantial sums on the gamble. With the exchange rates set in the 1940s becoming increasingly over- or undervalued, countries began to run persistent deficits or surpluses and the resulting global imbalance eventually tore the system apart in a series of shuddering crises from the late 1960s. The gamble on which way an exchange rate would move under pressure became a sure bet.

With the abandonment of the global pegged exchange rate system in the early 1970s under the pressure of more integrated capital markets, a new solution to the trilemma had to be chosen. The United States, as the world's largest economy, abandoned both controls on capital flows and pegged exchange rates in order to retain policy sovereignty. Many developing states could not manage the fluctuations in income and finances that would arise from a floating exchange rate and were willing to follow US monetary policy by pegging to the US dollar. By the late 1970s, the instability of the US dollar in global markets drove many of these states to adopt a more complex regime that stabilised their exchange rate in terms of a basket of currencies instead of just the US dollar. This allowed greater exchange rate flexibility and thus some increased policy sovereignty. On the other hand, by the 1990s many emerging economies, particularly in Asia and South America, had adopted a bilateral peg to the US dollar to benefit from exchange rate stability and the sound monetary policy of the United States, which encouraged confidence in their economic management. As a result, they were able to attract huge inflows of foreign investment, but this boom soon foundered on inadequate institutional foundations. After financial and currency crises in a series of emerging markets in Europe, Latin America and Asia in the 1990s, many of these states moved to a new solution with greater exchange rate flexibility to absorb balance-of-payments shocks and allow more policy sovereignty as they targeted their economic policies at achieving low inflation.

A vital exception to this trend was the People's Republic of China, which pegged its exchange rate to the US dollar in 1994 and then sustained that rate throughout a decade of dramatic economic growth and trade liberalisation. In the context of the trilemma, China's solution was to retain policy sovereignty by imposing tight controls on flows of capital in and out of the country. As China's competitiveness increased, the demand for their products grew and foreign companies flooded into the Chinese economy, bringing substantial and growing amounts of investment. The result was that the 1994 exchange rate soon appeared undervalued and China accumulated huge foreign exchange reserves. In 2005, along with some liberalisation of financial markets, China moved to a slightly more flexible rate to allow appreciation of the yuan. The huge Chinese balance-of-payments surplus nevertheless continued to accumulate, contributing to the global imbalance that prompted the 2007–8 international financial crisis.

For European states, the solution was to try to retain exchange rate stability on a regional basis with some controls on capital and some loss of policy sovereignty as a pathway to economic and monetary union during the 1980s. The foundation of the euro in 1999 appeared to mark the formal adoption of a solution, where policy sovereignty over interest rates was abandoned to a single European monetary policy, exchange rates became irrevocably fixed by adopting a common currency, and liberalised capital markets promoted regional growth. Fiscal policy, however, remained a national prerogative and attempts to co-ordinate borrowing limits failed to bring about the convergence in broader economic policy required for a fully stable monetary union. The Greek financial crisis of 2010 showed the frailty of Europe's solution to the trilemma. That country's huge deficits required enormous bailouts and support from the International Monetary Fund (IMF) as well as the European Central Bank in order to ensure the continuation of the euro in Greece and to prevent market panic spreading to other faltering member states such as Ireland, Portugal and Spain. Ensuring national economic policy sovereignty while retaining exchange rate stability in the context of open capital markets remained elusive.

Basic trends in international economic relations

Figure 1.2 shows the annual rate of growth of world output from 1950–2008. The period from 1950–73 stands out as an era when overall growth rates were relatively high historically, reaching levels not attained again. This is known as the Long Boom of economic growth as many economies recovered from the Second World War, liberalised their trade and embarked on expansionist regimes that prioritised full employment and economic prosperity. For developed countries in North America and Europe, this era of job security, expanding educational opportunities, technological innovation and rising productivity is seen in retrospect as a golden era. The decade of prosperity in the 1960s was accompanied by pressure for social change to rectify internal inequities – including movements such as second-wave feminism, the civil rights movement and environmentalism – as well as supporting social experiments such as the 'hippy' counterculture. These movements all had earlier roots (such as the nineteenth-century suffragettes in the case of feminism) and political contexts such as the Vietnam War provoked many Americans and Europeans to challenge authority, but the economic environment was also an important factor. It was easier to 'drop out' of the economic system when returning to employment was expected to be unproblematic. Poorer countries, as we shall see, did not share equally in this era of prosperity, although advances were made in attaining greater self-determination through decolonisation. Some countries in East Asia took advantage of the growth of international trade to embark on sustained growth trajectories, copying some of the sources of Japan's economic 'miracle' based on high savings rates, adoption of existing technology and high labour productivity. This was also the Cold War era, which divided the world into blocs of communism and capitalism. Communist states in

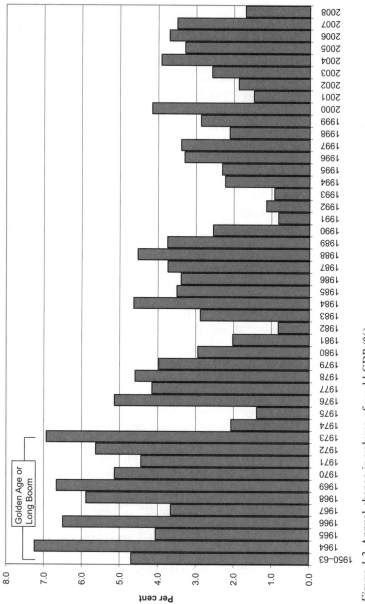

Figure 1.2 Annual change in volume of world GDP (%)

Source: WTO, *International Trade Statistics 2009*, 2009

Europe and Asia had a limited engagement with the global economic system and devised more limited systems of exchange not based on capitalist gains from trade, but based on the development of heavy industry and self-sufficiency. After the 1950s, growth in these economies tended to slow down as they reached the frontiers of their technological development.

The promise of sustained progress in developed countries was abruptly interrupted by the oil crisis of 1973–4, although growth resumed at more than 5 per cent p.a. by 1976. Another shock from the oil crisis at the start of the 1980s marked a second contraction in the global growth rate, but again, recovery was swift as financial markets were liberalised, China re-entered the international economy and the second era of globalisation began. At the start of the 1990s a downturn associated with the end of asset market booms in housing and stock prices in the developed world was followed by weaker recovery as emerging markets entered a decade of turmoil. The collapse of the dot.com boom in share markets and terrorist attacks on the Twin Towers in New York in 2001 negatively affected growth at the start of the next decade, and this time sustained recovery was interrupted by the onset of the financial crisis in 2007–8.

Behind these changes in the pace of growth in output there were significant variations in price. Figure 1.3 indicates the trend in inflation for advanced economies by presenting the average annual changes in the consumer price index for Organization for Economic Cooperation and Development (OECD) members from 1970 and for the UK and the US from 1956. In a long-term perspective, inflation during the Long Boom of the 1960s appears modest compared with the inflationary decades of the 1970s and early 1980s when repeated oil crises and monetary expansion prompted soaring inflation, particularly in the UK. From the 1980s, inflation was moderated by the application of monetarist policies that targeted growth of the money supply, and later by other policies targeted more directly at controlling inflation. Over the twenty years from the mid-1980s to the mid-2000s, the variability of inflation and output growth declined dramatically in most major industrial countries, a phenomenon that became known as 'The Great Moderation'. Its causes included the development of technologies that reduced friction and risk in business transactions, freer trade and payments and more effective monetary policy that constrained inflation without sacrificing growth. The world economy seemed to be entering a new phase of stability, but the permanence of the Great Moderation was abruptly challenged by the financial crisis of 2007–9 when the global recession prompted deflation in the United States for the first time since the Second World War.

International trade grew faster than world gross domestic product (GDP) from 1970–80 and again from the early 1990s. The first round of rapid trade

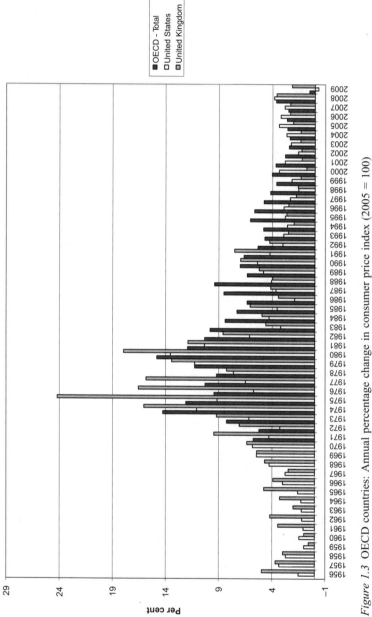

Figure 1.3 OECD countries: Annual percentage change in consumer price index (2005 = 100)

Source: OECD

growth was driven by soaring commodity prices and falling rates of output growth, while the second round of acceleration reflects the 'second globalisation' of the international economy driven by technological innovation and foreign investment. Figure 1.4 also shows that for developing economies, exports were larger relative to total output, partly driven by rising commodity prices particularly for oil producers. The US economy, as the largest in the world, was relatively independent of international trade, while conversely European states were very open to trade, particularly with each other, due to the deliberate process of European integration.

Figure 1.5 shows the consistent domination of developed states in international trade. The main factor eroding this position in the 1970s was the oil crisis, which increased the share held by nations belonging to the Organization of Petroleum Exporting Countries (OPEC), although this effect was reversed by the late 1980s. What is also clear is that the relative position of developing economies in world trade receded during the long post-war boom from 1955–73 and that it took another forty years to recover the relative position of the 1950s. This trend was mainly due to falling terms of trade on agricultural products and was reversed through the expansion of manufactured exports by developing countries, in particular China and other economies in East Asia. Agricultural protectionism in developed countries further constrained the participation of less developed economies in the gains from international trade. Developed states traded overwhelmingly among themselves, so that 70 per cent to 80 per cent of exports to advanced economies originated in other advanced economies. The unequal participation of rich and poor countries is a key theme of post-war international economic relations.

After trade in goods and services, the most visible form of international economic exchange is the movement of people. In the immediate post-war period, of course, the disruptions of war and changes to political borders led to large-scale migration. For example, about 690,000 people moved to the new state of Israel from 1948–51. Table 1.2 shows that the number of international migrants doubled from 1960 to 1990, and that by 2000, 175 million people were living in countries other than where they were born. Recorded migrants accounted for about 3 per cent of the world's population in 2000, compared with 2.1 per cent in 1910, according to the UN *World Economic and Social Survey* (2004). During the 1960s the number of international migrants grew at an average annual rate of 0.7 per cent, but this rose to 2 per cent in the 1970s and 4.3 per cent p.a. in the 1980s, before subsiding to 1.3 per cent in the 1990s. The peak from 1980 to 1990 was primarily due to the break up of the Soviet Union, which created about 27 million migrants through border changes.[4] By far the largest single destination was the United States, where, according to the UN, by 2010

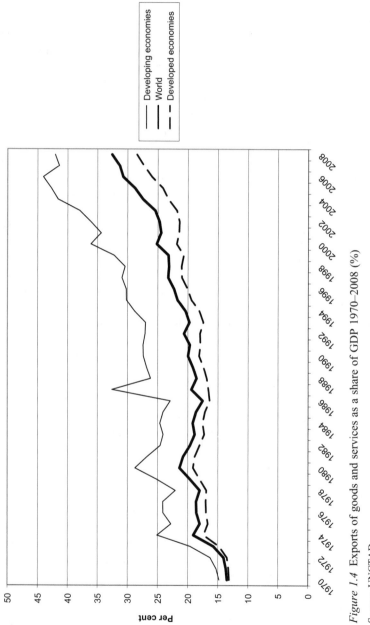

Figure 1.4 Exports of goods and services as a share of GDP 1970–2008 (%)

Source: UNCTAD

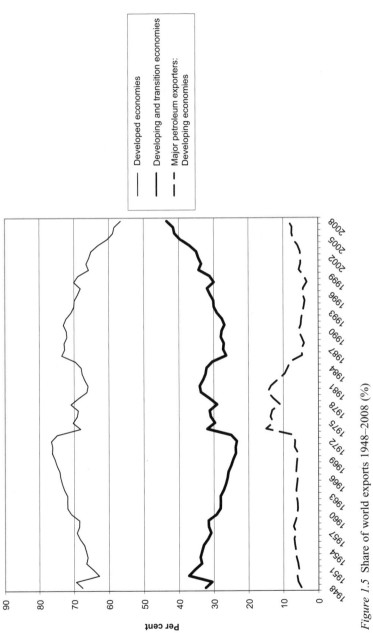

Figure 1.5 Share of world exports 1948–2008 (%)

Source: UNCTAD

about 43 million recorded migrants lived, with Russia a distant second place with 12.3 million. The large share for Asia included foreign workers who moved to many Middle East and Persian Gulf states after the oil boom in 1973 and also flows of labour into the construction and service industries of rapidly growing economies such as Singapore.

It is also clear in Table 1.2 that, unlike international trade, the location of international migrants was split fairly evenly between developed countries and developing countries until the 1990s, when the break-up of the Soviet Union increased the share of the developed world. As we shall see, however, most migrants to richer economies also originated in the developed world, while developing-country migrants tended to move to neighbouring developing economies. Also, migrants as a share of the total population doubled from 4 per cent to 8 per cent for developed countries (excluding the Soviet Union) but halved from 2 per cent to 1 per cent for developing countries. In this sense, international migration did not help redistribute surplus labour from poor to rich countries in the way that had characterised the migration of unskilled labour from crowded European economies to North America, South America and Oceania in the globalisation of the late nineteenth century.

Closely related to movements of goods, people and ideas was the extension of enterprises from one country to another. This process of foreign

Table 1.2 Stock of international migrants (millions)

	1960	1970	1980	1990	2000
World	75.9	81.5	99.8	154.0	174.9
Developed countries (incl. USSR)	32.1	38.3	47.7	89.7	110.3
Developed countries (excl. USSR)	29.1	35.2	44.5	59.3	80.8
Developing countries	43.8	43.2	52.1	64.3	64.6
SHARE of world total (%)					
Developed countries (incl. USSR)	42.3	47.0	47.8	58.2	63.1
Developed countries (excl. USSR)	38.5	43.2	44.5	38.6	46.2
Developing countries	57.7	53.0	52.2	41.8	36.9
SHARE by region (%)					
Africa	11.9	12.1	14.1	10.5	9.3
Asia	38.6	34.5	32.4	27.1	25.0
Latin America and Caribbean	7.9	7.1	6.1	4.5	3.4
Northern America	16.5	16.0	18.1	17.9	23.3
Oceania	2.8	3.7	3.8	3.1	3.3
Europe	18.4	22.9	22.2	17.1	18.8
Former USSR	3.8	3.8	3.3	19.7	16.9

Source: UN World Economic and Social Survey, 2004

direct investment, where the investor retains an element of control over the target investment, was a prominent feature of post-war international economic relations, spreading economic activity, transferring working practices and homogenising consumer options. As in the case of trade and migration, the general trend was toward companies in richer economies tending to relocate to or invest in similarly wealthy economies to exploit their consumer market. This was particularly true for US multinational corporations in the 1960s and 1970s, as they moved abroad to the UK and continental Europe to take advantage of rising incomes for goods and services. This strategy allowed US firms to exploit their managerial or technological advantages and overcome barriers to trade, so that this form of investment tended to replace exports of finished goods rather than increase trade directly, although the company might import parts or machinery from the source country. Similarly, in the 2000s some Chinese companies moved production to the new, lower wage members of the EU to overcome trade barriers. Another motivation for outward FDI, which links the developing and developed world, is resource-seeking. A resource-seeking company might be a manufacturer seeking cheaper labour for assembly, as was the case for a range of investors in newly industrialising economies in East Asia in the 1960s and 1970s, where labour was relatively cheap compared to the home market. The toys, clothes or shoes would then be exported to wealthier markets for consumption, thus increasing international trade. Mining or oil exploration companies invested in resource-rich developing economies such as Brazil or oil-producing states in the Middle East. Again, this form of FDI was trade-enhancing since the production was brought into the international market.

Foreign investment generated new products, opportunities and working practices but could also have detrimental effects if large foreign firms crowded out local entrepreneurs or merely exploited cheap, unskilled labour without transferring skills. While in the nineteenth century, the benefits of foreign investment were relatively uncontested, during the post-war years the challenges to local government sovereignty and development goals as well as the transfer of cultural traits such as consumer products or working practices prompted controversy over the role of international companies. In 1967, Servan-Schreiber's famous critique of US FDI, *Le Défi Americain* (*The American Challenge*), claimed that the invasion of American companies would reduce Europe to a mere branch of the US economy. Seven years later Barnet and Muller castigated US multinational corporations (MNCs) for their colonising tendencies in developing economies such as Latin America. In the 1980s, similar fears were expressed about Japanese companies opening in Europe and the United States and the challenge this posed to working practices and labour relations.[5] In the 2000s outward investment of Chinese companies in oil- and resource-rich African states prompted a literature of the 'China threat' linking economic expansion to political ambitions. While all international economic relations provoke some level of disagreement – as we saw in the case of trade – the dramatic increase in international movement of people and capital during the post-war period and the impact on livelihoods, culture and economic prospects have certainly proved of enduring controversy.

Even more dramatic than the investment of firms in global production and distribution processes was the explosion of flows of international financial capital from the early 1960s. This form of investment is sometimes known as 'portfolio' investment, since it entails the purchase and sale of assets that are represented by pieces of paper that could be held in a portfolio. This category includes company shares, government and corporate bonds, certificates of deposit, derivatives and other complex financial assets. The development of offshore financial markets after 1945 began first in London from the late 1950s before spreading through a range of global international financial centres as exchange controls were relaxed and the opportunities for financial innovation accelerated. Investors sought to protect themselves from interest rate and exchange rate risk in the 1970s and 1980s, and the market met their needs through new and more complex financial products. There were periodic setbacks to the flow of financial capital, such as after the Latin American debt crisis of 1982 or the emerging market crises of the 1990s, but the resilience and pace of innovation in these markets drove renewed growth in the value of international financial flows. During the 1990s and 2000s the skills of financial engineering and the integration of markets allowed ever more complex products to be developed, which appeared to spread risk while retaining returns through deep and apparently liquid international financial markets. By the mid-1990s the value of international debt securities issued by financial institutions themselves outweighed the securities issued by governments and corporations combined. Chapter 7 will show how the volume and complexity of international financial products was a key element in the financial crisis of 2007–9.

The chapters in this book are arranged broadly chronologically to allow a sense of the development of the international economy alongside the changing organisation of international economic relations. These developments, however, do not fall tidily into a strict chronology, so there is some overlap in the periods covered by each chapter. The goal is to provide an overview of how national economies interacted and the forces that shaped that interaction, rather than an account of the growth of national or regional economies themselves. Nor is this book a historiography of the global economy, but rather a survey of developments to provide readers with the context for more in depth analysis. A particular emphasis is placed on economic policy-making at national, regional and supranational level, as well as on the ideological foundations that shaped the multilateral institutions that governed those relations. The first two chapters establish how the international economic system was re-designed after the turmoil of the Great Depression of the 1930s and the global conflict of 1939–45. Stress is placed on the importance of the historical legacy of inter-linked economic and strategic conflict for the design of the post-war system. While the goals of post-war planners were ambitious and inclusive, the reality fell somewhat short of the ideal, so international economic relations fell into regional systems to restrain capital flows while liberalising trade to retain national sovereignty under a pegged exchange rate regime. The system eventually foundered under a range of stresses discussed in Chapter 4, and the international economy entered its first major post-war period of instability and crisis. Growth slowed, jobs were lost and inflation soared, shattering the Keynesian consensus that had underpinned the Bretton Woods system. The legacy of the volatile 1970s was felt particularly keenly by developing economies lured into heavy sovereign borrowing to correct balance-of-payments problems. The resulting debt crisis prompted a concerted effort to harness global financial activity through common risk-based quality standards for international banking. By the mid-1980s, as Chapter 5 shows, a new liberal ideology prevailed in many nations and market reforms prompted the relaxation of controls on flows of international capital. Over the next decade, this process of globalisation spread more widely, notably with the re-emergence of the dynamic Chinese economy into the international system, but Chapter 6 shows that a series of crises in emerging economies from the middle of the decade revealed the fragile nature of many financial institutions and the dangers of contagion in this increasingly integrated global financial market. The threat that unstable boom economies posed to the global economic system seemed to be overcome in the 2000s as several emerging market economies appeared destined to play a more central global role based on sustained growth. This optimism was also soon shattered by the onset of the most damaging global financial crisis of the post-war period in 2007–8, which is discussed in Chapter 7.

2 Rebuilding the international economic system 1945–50

The origins of the post-war international economic system lay in the two decades of turmoil that preceded the outbreak of the Second World War and the commitment of all states to avoid such a calamity in the future. Governments around the world were committed to restoring jobs and prosperity for their populations after the thirty years of upheaval since 1914, and a smoothly functioning international economic system was considered crucial to achieving this goal. There were two main lessons that policy-makers gleaned from the period of crisis that swept through the international economy during the 1920s and 1930s. The failure to achieve a lasting peace through the Treaty of Versailles was blamed in large part on the economic complications arising from the financing of the First World War and the economic sanctions and reparations imposed on Germany in its aftermath. A first motivation for greater co-operation, therefore, was to avoid the cycle of war debts whose repayment was dependent on extracting reparations from the losers of the war. Second, the depth and extent of the Great Depression of the 1930s, which destabilised governments and spread misery throughout the globe, was blamed partly on the lack of effective co-operation in sustaining international trade and inattention to the importance of a carefully monitored system to ensure exchange rate stability.[1] Traders and investors would be reassured by a stable exchange rate system that removed an element of risk from international economic transactions. Competitive currency devaluations and trade tariffs used by many governments to insulate themselves from the global downturn in the 1930s were labelled 'beggar thy neighbour' policies. It was widely believed that these responses had created the downward spiral of the Great Depression, and so they needed to be prevented by an external framework to monitor each country's policies and impose some sort of sanction for disruptive behaviour that threatened systemic stability. The independent nationalistic model of the inter-war period, led by America's isolationism, was to be replaced by greater co-ordination and US leadership.

Reflecting the politics of the war, planning for the organisation of the international economy was essentially an Anglo-American project during the 1940s. The American administration used its economic and strategic strength to lead the process in partnership with the UK. At the outset of war in Europe in 1939, the US government remained detached from the conflict due to the legacy of isolationism. The Johnson Act of 1934 forbade the US from lending to the countries in arrears on their First World War debts, and the 1935 Neutrality Act prevented sales of arms. From June 1940 after the fall of France to German forces, the British Cabinet agreed that the threat was so great that all UK resources should be expended immediately rather than budgeting for a three-year effort. Still the US government resisted providing aid until after Roosevelt was re-elected in November 1940. The next month, a personal appeal from Churchill prompted the discovery of an obscure 1892 Act that allowed the lease of armaments for purposes 'essential to the defence of the USA'. Roosevelt pledged to 'eliminate the dollar sign' in US war aid so as not to accumulate war debts and he began a campaign to persuade the American public that supporting the Allied forces to stem the tide of Nazism was in the American interest.

This commitment was the genesis of what became known as Lend-Lease, which lay at the foundation of the planning for the post-war international economic structure. American factories would produce munitions, the US government bought them and 'leased' them to the UK and allies. Lend-Lease became law on 11 March 1941, and over the course of the war this aid amounted to US$44 billion, of which $30 billion went to the British empire (mostly to the UK) and $10 billion to the Soviet Union. Of this total, 65 per cent was in the form of munitions and 35 per cent for food. The price for these goods was not paid in cash, since this raised the spectre of unrecoverable war debts, but some ill-defined 'consideration' to be determined in the near future. In essence the American administration boldly eliminated the war debt cycle that had so plagued the settlement of the First World War in the interests of avoiding a repeat of the Great Depression. In return for this generosity they expected the allied powers to co-operate in their vision of the post-war system based on freer trade and payments that would help to ensure global prosperity and ensure a lasting peace.

The US goal was to reconstruct a multilateral system of world trade where barriers to trade and payments were minimised (although not eliminated) and non-discriminatory. If all countries were treated equally in trade, then this would minimise conflict and would ensure American companies and farmers gained fair access to markets overseas. This system had two requirements. First, it required external convertibility of currencies; traders needed to be able to buy and sell currencies on a foreign exchange market.

Only by having convertibility can traders use a surplus earned from sales to one country to offset a deficit with another. Having convertible currencies allows producers to sell in markets where they gain the best price and consumers to buy goods from countries with the cheapest and most desirable products. This greatly increased the potential volume of international trade over a bilateral system where each country had to balance its accounts against each trading partner. Second, a multilateral system meant that any obstacles to trade should be applied equally to all countries, which required the elimination of discriminatory higher tariffs on imports from, for example, the United States. This second requirement further ensured that trade flowed in accordance with relative price considerations only. The project of trade liberalisation and currency convertibility were linked, therefore, as elements necessary to achieve a more efficient system of trade that would ensure the best prospects for growth and prosperity.

The British response to these proposals was cautious, partly because the government was preoccupied with the war. During the 1930s the UK had developed a network of preferential tariff rates for commonwealth and empire states known as Imperial Preference, and they were loathe to abandon this without further safeguards that the US would indeed pursue growth and full employment rather than lead the world into depression as had occurred in the 1930s. Having sold most foreign assets as part of the war effort and diverted production to munitions, the British government was also aware that they would require continued controls on currency, production and consumption to achieve economic recovery after the war ended. Nevertheless, the wartime coalition government was fully committed to full employment over the longer term, which would require a revival of international trade and sustained growth, consistent with American priorities.

The terms of the post-war settlement were further defined by formal agreement between the US and the UK in the Atlantic Charter of July 1941 and the Mutual Aid Agreement of February 1942. The Atlantic Charter was signed in a dramatic and secret meeting between Churchill and Roosevelt on a ship off the coast of Newfoundland. Churchill ran a considerable risk in sailing across the Atlantic, but the personal meeting between the two leaders was deemed necessary to confirm the commitments on each side. The Charter provided a wide-ranging vision of the post-war world, including self-determination of political borders, but it also set out the joint commitment to a new multilateral economic order. Some debate arose over trade discrimination, as it was impossible for Churchill to promise to abandon the bilateral treaties that made up the preferential trade system for the commonwealth and empire. Points 4 and 5 of the Charter were as follows, with the last minute amendment (underlined in the text below) reassuring the British side that Imperial Preference could continue:

Fourth, they will endeavor, <u>with due respect for their existing obligations</u>, to further the enjoyment by all States, great or small, victor or vanquished, of access, on equal terms, to the trade and to the raw materials of the world which are needed for their economic prosperity;

Fifth, they desire to bring about the fullest collaboration between all nations in the economic field with the object of securing, for all, improved labor standards, economic advancement and social security . . .

The Mutual Aid Agreement seven months later formalised the terms of Lend-Lease, defining the 'consideration' due from the UK and allies in return for US aid. Embodied in the agreement was the commitment to expand production, employment and trade, eliminate discrimination (gradually), reduce tariffs and not burden commerce with war debts. Article VII committed the allies to meet to establish a new international trade and payments system, aimed at:

. . . expansion, by appropriate international and domestic measures, of production, employment, and the exchange and consumption of goods, which are the material foundations of the liberty and welfare of all peoples; to the elimination of all forms of discriminatory treatment in international commerce, and to the reduction of tariffs and other trade barriers.

Even before the Mutual Aid Agreement was finalised, planning for a global system had already begun on both sides of the Atlantic. The plans, although developed independently, shared several characteristics. The first was that some form of credit or liquidity would be needed for countries to survive short-term downturns without recourse to the kinds of beggar-thy-neighbour policies that had been so harmful during the inter-war period. Short-term external fluctuations should be met by temporary solutions rather than by tariffs or currency devaluations that had longer-term effects and provoked dangerous retaliation that threatened systemic stability. The second shared feature was that both sets of planners sought to promote a system of multilateral payments in which countries could achieve growth and avoid crisis at high levels of domestic employment. In sum, both sought a fixed exchange rate system policed by an international institution that also provided credit as a cushion against short-term balance-of-payments problems. This cushion should give countries the confidence to free up controls on trade and payments to allow the greatest potential for growth in the international economy.

In Washington, Harry Dexter White of the US Treasury had been working on proposals and took the leadership of American planning. His proposal was initially for two new international institutions: a Stabilisation Fund and a Bank for Reconstruction. The Fund would hold about US$5 billion contributed by member countries, which would be available for short-term loans to offset temporary balance-of-payments difficulties. Without access to such credit or lender of last resort, countries in deficit would otherwise have to contract their domestic economies, stop buying foreign goods or devalue their currency in order to boost exports and curtail imports. These were all responses that had contributed to the Great Depression, and so the goal of the Fund was to ensure the smoother functioning of the international economy and to retain the prospects for growth that arose from international trade. The Bank for Reconstruction was to have access to US$10 billion worth of gold and local currencies contributed by members for reconstruction, relief and economic recovery. Such an amount was clearly not enough to repair global destruction from the war, but was merely intended to act as seed money to attract private capital. It could also provide counter-cyclical longer-term lending to offset global downturns and might be used to stabilise raw material prices. As the planning process developed, the Bank receded from discussion and funding the immediate post-war reconstruction was pushed further down the agenda.

In the UK, the greatest economic mind in the country was engaged in post-war planning. John Maynard Keynes had been an influential critic of the Versailles settlement after the First World War and of the return to the Gold Standard, which overvalued the pound sterling in 1925 and required a deflationary policy in the UK that damaged growth.[2] It was therefore natural that Keynes would lead the planning to avoid these mistakes in the future. The Keynes Plan was much more ambitious and imaginative than the White Plan, although it sought the same goals of exchange rate stability and multilateralism. Drawing on the lesson of the US recession pulling the world into depression in the 1930s, Keynes put more emphasis on insulating or defending countries from economic changes in other countries that were beyond their control. Reflecting on the failure of the inter-war pegged exchange rate system, he also sought to combine stable exchange rates with domestic economic expansion. Keynes devised an International Clearing Union (ICU) as an automatic way for countries to balance their bilateral surpluses and deficits with other countries. Surpluses and deficits in the balance of payments of members would be combined in credits and debits in the accounting books of the ICU denominated in a new international unit of account, called Bancor. By using a new unit of account rather than a particular currency, the ICU did not need any contributions up front from members and provided a full and automatic multilateral clearing system. The ICU would also offer credit to each member in a form similar to a bank overdraft. Each member's entitlement was linked to the country's pre-war share of global trade and the total credit available amounted to the equivalent of US$26 billion. The Bancor balances of surplus members would be available to be borrowed by deficit members. With such large credit facilities countries could eliminate exchange control, maintain stable exchange rates and pursue domestic expansion without worrying about their foreign balance. Keynes' emphasis reflected his concern that domestic expansion and full employment should not be inhibited by deficits in a country's balance of payments. He assumed that the problem after the war would be deflation spreading from an American recession (as it was in the 1930s), so his plan was biased toward allowing countries to run inflationary expansionist policies to offset this pressure.

The difference between the two plans clearly reflected the fact that the UK expected to be a debtor after the war and the US expected to be a creditor. First, the size of total credit was US$5 billion in the White Plan compared with US$26 billion in the Keynes Plan. The Fund required countries to contribute up front while the ICU credits in Bancor were created freely as accounting entities. White put the onus of adjustment on debtors since loans from the Fund were temporary and would need to be repaid. No action was to be taken against countries running surpluses. The ICU, however, charged interest on both surpluses and deficits to induce surplus countries to pursue expansionary policies rather than encouraging deficit countries to contract their growth.

In his classic analysis, Gardner identified three key aspects in both of the plans that ultimately undermined the functioning of the final system.[3] First, both tended to ignore the problem of how countries would finance the transition from wartime to peacetime and reconstruct their infrastructure and industry as well as their trade links. This was particularly true as the Bank proposal receded in importance, since both the Fund and the ICU were predicated on all members having open economies without fundamental external or internal imbalances. They were both designed to deal with short-term fluctuations rather than the structural problems that would emerge after the war. This was partly because of the huge and immeasurable task that it was clear global reconstruction would entail, and because any new institution of global economic governance might never function properly if it were burdened with this task. A second flaw was that both plans provided credit for short-term imbalances – but what if these were misdiagnosed and problems were actually longer term or more structural? How would countries be encouraged to make the fundamental adjustments required to regain equilibrium and at what point would it be appropriate to change the exchange rate to reflect underlying permanent changes in competitiveness? The final and related feature was liquidity; credits needed to be large and freely accessible enough to give governments the confidence to abandon their controls on convertibility and give up the freedom to change their exchange rate, but at the same time the total amount needed to be acceptable to the American people, who did not want their country to have to bail out the world's debtors. These tensions between British and American priorities were the subject of a series of international summits from 1943 that gradually included a wider and wider range of countries, culminating in the famous Bretton Woods meeting of forty-four countries in 1944.

Bretton Woods and the founding of the IMF

The Keynes Plan and the White Plan were published separately in April 1943 and a series of meetings ensued as promised under Article VII of the Mutual Aid Agreement. From 15 September to 9 October 1943 representatives of thirty countries met in Washington to develop a consensus that was finally published as the Joint Statement by Experts on the Establishment of an International Monetary Fund (IMF) in April 1944. The outcome followed the White Plan much more closely than the Keynes Plan. The ICU was in the end too ambitious for American politicians to contemplate seriously. Since the ICU overdrafts were denominated in Bancor rather than national currencies all countries in the world could theoretically use their credit to buy goods from the United States. In essence this would require the United States to provide up to US$23 billion in credit to the rest of the world (US$26 billion less the US overdraft entitlement of US$3 billion), an amount that would not be accepted by the American public.

With a joint agreement on principles for a Fund-based solution, representatives of sixteen countries met from 23–30 June 1944 in Atlantic City, New Jersey, to iron out remaining problems, including amendments to the Joint Statement. At this point the Bank for Reconstruction had resurfaced and details were hammered out. Finally, the major summit was held during the first three weeks of July 1944 at the Mount Washington Hotel in Bretton Woods, New Hampshire, where 730 delegates, representing 44 members of United and Associated Nations agreed the framework for the international monetary system. The Bretton Woods agreement established the IMF and the International Bank for Reconstruction and Development (IBRD).

The Fund followed White's model, although it was slightly larger with US$8.8 billion of contributions, of which the main contributors were the United States with $2.75 billion (31 per cent of the total), the UK with $1.3 billion (15 per cent of the total), China with $550 million, France with $450 million, and India with $400 million. The size of these 'quotas' was determined according to a formula guided by pre-war trade and reserves. One quarter of each member's quota had to be paid in gold or US dollars and the rest in the country's own currency. These funds were then available to be borrowed by members when their balance of payments fell into deficit. Each country could draw out 25 per cent of their initial contribution quite freely, but to draw more from the Fund required an application to the Executive Board of the IMF, which could impose conditions on further borrowing, such as policies to correct internal prices and incomes. This IMF 'conditionality' and the uncertainty about what it might involve discouraged members from using the Fund in its first few years, particularly since voting rights of members of the Executive Board were determined by the size of each member's quota, so the United States dominated. Members were only allowed to alter their exchange rate if the Executive Board determined that they were in 'fundamental disequilibrium', although this was left undefined. In essence, the system was a pegged exchange rate regime where all currencies were valued in terms of US dollar. Exchange rates could fluctuate only 1 per cent on either side of their par value with the dollar. The dollar alone was pegged to a gold value of US$35 per ounce. Under such a pegged rate system, any adjustment to correct the balance of payments must fall on internal prices and incomes or the national foreign exchange reserves, although access to the IMF's resources were meant to temper any negative effects from short-term imbalances.

The IBRD was a more modest enterprise, with the ability to call up to US$10 billion from members but with strict limitations on its lending and a focus on generating private investment rather than taking on reconstruction itself. It made some initial loans (totalling about US$500 million) to Western Europe but was taken over by US Marshall Aid in 1948, and its activities came to emphasise development rather than recovery. The IBRD was not the solution to the transition period from war to peace, and the IMF was specifically not to lend for relief or reconstruction arising from the war. Given the structural dislocation of most economies, the framers of the IMF recognised that most members would not be able to abandon their external controls immediately after ratification, and so Article XIV of the IMF anticipated a period of three to five years of continued exchange controls. After five years members had to report annually on why they still needed exchange controls. We shall see that the failure to resolve the method of transition and recovery had a profound impact on how these two new institutions actually operated. There was no final deadline for abandoning exchange controls or trade restrictions, and in the end the former were retained for a further thirteen years after the end of the war.

The institutions established at Bretton Woods represented an enormous achievement of global consensus on a complex issue that infringed on national sovereignty. As the war drew to a close first in Europe and then in Asia, the passion for global co-operation that had generated the United Nations as well as the IMF began to cool with the onset of the Cold War. At the outset, the agreements included the USSR, but as the Eastern Bloc consolidated after the end of the war they subsequently withdrew. More fundamentally, the underlying principles of the Bretton Woods agreements became increasingly contested as it became clear that protectionist measures were necessary to provide the foundation for reconstruction and recovery. Freer trade and currency convertibility seemed like costly luxuries for populations struggling to find housing and food in the economic and social dislocation following the war. Both on the American and the British side, ratification of the Articles of Agreement was delayed as more urgent pressures on policy took precedence.

As predicted, the UK was in a difficult position from which to recover in 1945, having sold its foreign assets, which had traditionally generated income, and with few resources devoted to producing goods for export. Britain had also accumulated over £2.4 billion of debt to a range of commonwealth and empire partners as part of their war expenditure overseas, mainly in India. All of Europe sought the raw materials and engineering goods to restore industry and infrastructure, and the US and Canada were the main sources of these essential imports. However, until the world's industries were recovered these economies had little to sell to America to generate the dollars to buy these essential imports. This created a shortage of US and Canadian dollars as countries scrambled to earn these currencies or to convert any other foreign exchange they could to dollars. As a result, no European country (and very few countries outside Europe) could afford to allow its currency to be convertible to US dollars. The dollar shortage meant that the goal of convertibility and multilateral trade appeared to be postponed indefinitely.

The US curtailed the supply of Lend-Lease aid abruptly at the end of the war, even with orders outstanding. This created an urgent need for aid or loans, for Britain in particular. Keynes embarked on a mission to negotiate a loan in Washington in 1946 but found the Americans relatively unsympathetic and ready to use their leverage to hasten Britain's adoption of the principles of multilateralism, convertibility and freer trade. After several months of acrimonious negotiation, which helped to hasten Keynes' death soon after, the Anglo-American Loan Agreement was signed in July 1946. Britain received a line of credit of US$3.75 billion at 2 per cent p.a. to be repaid over 50 years. As a condition, the British government was committed to try to eliminate their debts to India and other empire and commonwealth countries through negotiation, to ratify the Articles of Agreement for the IMF and the IBRD and, more riskily, to make sterling freely convertible to US dollars and all other European currencies within twelve months. The Anglo-American Loan Agreement thus cut the transition period for the UK from three to five years to one year only. At the time, the convertibility condition attracted less attention than the commitment to negotiate the cancellation of Britain's war debts to the empire and commonwealth, but in the longer term this clause proved to be a major turning point for the organisation of the international monetary system. In the meantime, negotiations on a trade institution to mirror the IMF were underway.

International Trade Organisation

As was noted above, a driving motivation for planners during the war was to restore freer trade as well as a more stable payments system. Indeed, trade had a higher profile in both the Atlantic Charter and the Mutual Aid Agreement than the monetary system. In September 1943 the Americans and the British agreed on the need to establish an international code of practice for trade that would be enforced by an international agency. Officials met in September 1945 in London to draft 'Proposals for Consideration by an International Conference on Trade and Employment' to design an International Trade Organisation (ITO) analogous to the IMF.

The extent of co-operation over trade, however, proved to be much more limited and contested than was the case for the IMF. This was for several reasons. Politically, lobby groups for trade protection were strong and clearly identifiable, whereas the monetary system's costs and benefits were more dispersed. Trade liberalisation could be a more difficult policy to sell to voters who viewed foreign imports as a challenge to their own jobs. The previous section noted the importance of Imperial Preference for British economic policy since it encouraged a market for British goods and enhanced access to raw materials. Imperial Preference also helped to define Britain's strategic place in the world at the end of the war as leader of the commonwealth, and so the system was politically difficult to abandon. Finally, the enthusiasm for collective co-ordinated policy arrangements had been strong in the early 1940s, but this impetus weakened with the onset of the Cold War and stronger dissenting voices from developing countries. As a result, the proposed ITO was never finally ratified, and the process identified a range of obstacles that continue to plague international trade policy today, including conflicts of interest between developed and developing countries.

By 1946 the terms of an ITO as envisaged by the core economic powers had emerged. The key principles were that there should be no new preferences on trade (thus allowing the continuation of Imperial Preference), any new reduction in tariffs should be on an unconditional most-favoured-nation basis (that is, applied equally to all trading partners) and that all members should have an obligation to enter into reciprocal negotiations when asked to lower tariffs. This last provision was to protect the interest of smaller economies that might have little bargaining power to even begin negotiations. The preliminary conference to establish an ITO took place in Geneva in 1947. Here a deadlock emerged between the UK and the United States, especially over non-discrimination and Imperial Preference, and the meeting adjourned without agreement. The conference moved to Havana, Cuba, in the winter of 1948 where the ITO charter was finally drafted.

At Havana, Anglo-American leadership was challenged by a range of developing countries. Australia, India, Brazil and Chile together argued that the proposals took inadequate account of the needs of developing countries for tariff protection to establish new manufacturing sectors. Many developing countries had advanced their industrialisation efforts during the disruption in Europe during the war and sought to continue this process. Sustained growth depended on a more diversified economy, but with European competitors re-emerging into the global market, the nascent industries in developing economies were under threat and required continued protection from the competition of foreign imports. This group of countries argued that development should be enshrined as a key goal of any ITO and also that this goal should be formally recognised as a joint responsibility of both rich and poor countries. This would allow developing economies to claim exceptions not only to rules on quotas and tariffs but also on discrimination to allow regional groups to promote development through preferential trade. The failure of either the US or the UK to ratify the Havana Charter for an ITO marked a key moment in the widening split between rich and poor nations that would become more evident in the ensuing decades and remains one of the most intractable problems in the international economy.

In the meantime, the Americans had drawn up a vague interim charter that was signed by the Geneva delegates in 1947, incorporating the general principles of the ITO. This was formalised as the General Agreement on Tariffs and Trade (GATT), and it merely established basic principles without a new institution. The aim was to allow the process of tariff reduction to be less formal, less confrontational and more pragmatic while the ITO was finalised. Participants were committed only to provisions that did not contravene their existing legislation, so they posed little threat to national governments. In the end, these general rules were all that was achievable and the ITO was never ratified by the advanced industrial countries. Regional progress on trade liberalisation was subsequently achieved through the European Payments Union (EPU) and OECD, but the GATT remained the main international mechanism for trade negotiations until the founding the World Trade Organisation (WTO) forty-eight years later in 1995.

Recovery of the international economy

In the end, it could be argued that the IMF and IBRD had little impact on the successful international economic recovery over the following decade since they never operated quite as planned. As noted above, these institutions themselves did not make provision for recovery. In 1946 the US reluctantly accepted responsibility for a loan to its closest ally, the UK, but the conditions in the end undermined their goals of global multilateralism. As the deadline for making sterling convertible on 15 July 1947 approached, British spending on the line of credit accelerated and countries hoarded sterling in anticipation of converting it to US dollars. The British concluded a series of bilateral agreements with a range of European states to ensure that they would hold a set amount of sterling, but in the end this was not enough to preclude a run on the pound when it was finally made convertible in July. Over the course of six weeks, British reserves were drained of hundreds of millions of US dollars, and they finally had to suspend convertibility on 20 August 1947. The main outcome of this episode was to highlight the dangers of premature convertibility and therefore remove the impetus both in Europe and the United States for an early adoption of the terms of the Bretton Woods agreements. A new path to post-war reconstruction as well as a new structure to restore international economic relations was needed.

By the winter of 1946–7 the American administration was growing concerned about the pace of recovery of Western Europe and the potential for a dissatisfied and demoralised population to turn to communist solutions to their difficulties. William Clayton was sent to tour European capitals, and he reported his views back to the President in May 1947. He warned that many states were at a tipping point where, if recovery did not accelerate, then the threat of communist revolution was very real. This prompted the President to launch a fresh aid initiative for Western Europe that would (similar to Lend-Lease) be in the national interest of the United States, this time in its fight against the Soviet Bloc. It was announced by Secretary of State General George Marshall at the Harvard commencement ceremony in June 1947 and came to be known as the Marshall Plan.

The American government's motivations were both political and economic. As Marshall claimed in his Harvard speech:

Europe's requirements for the next three or four years of foreign food and other essential products – principally from America – are so much greater than her present ability to pay that she must have substantial additional help or face economic, social and political deterioration of a very grave character . . . Aside from the demoralizing effect on the world at large and the possibilities of disturbances arising as a result of the desperation of the people concerned, the consequences to the economy of the United States should be apparent to all. It is logical that the United States should do whatever it is able to do to assist in the return of normal economic health in the world, without which there can be no political stability and no assured peace.

Politically, the American administration wanted to create a strong bulwark against the Eastern Bloc that would be a close ally of the United States. This required the governments of Western Europe to co-operate with each other to ensure that the expectations of their populations rose high enough to forestall the attractions of communism over the status quo. Economically, Europe was an important market for American production so a richer ally would further benefit the US economy. Economic and political integration of European states would ensure faster growth, greater prosperity and firmer resistance to communism. The terms of the aid aimed to encourage the achievement of these goals by forcing the recipients to submit a single co-ordinated bid for support. The need for co-operation had the added impact of excluding the Soviet Union from the aid since they refused to participate in a joint bid.

The proposals met with a cool response in Europe. The British did not view themselves as a mere component of a European state and the French suspected a conspiracy to reindustrialise (and remilitarise) Germany. Together they made arrangements to minimise the integration aspects of the programme while setting up a Committee for European Economic Cooperation (CEEC) to satisfy the American administration. The discussions at the CEEC were to be kept on a technical level to exclude ministers or officials with higher level strategic decision-making powers and so limit the momentum for economic or political integration. The technical committees would determine US dollar needs in their sectors and report to an Executive Committee of no more than five countries (which would exclude Germany) to ensure Anglo-French domination. The first bid in August 1947 was a thinly veiled set of sixteen separate programmes of aid with no provision for an ongoing joint organisation. This draft was rejected by the United States and replaced by a new proposal for an Organisation of European Economic Cooperation (OEEC) that would liaise with its US partner, the European Cooperation Administration, to distribute funds. This formed the European Recovery Programme, which eventually channelled

US$13 billion in grants and loans mainly to Western European countries between 1948 and 1951.

There is some controversy about the importance of the Marshall Plan to the recovery of Western Europe, which was clearly already under way. Milward (1984) noted that the size of the aid was small relative to the size of the economies involved and the size of the global imbalance, so its economic impact could not be that great. The total amount was about 5–10 per cent of the 1949 gross national product (GNP) of recipients, while flows each year from the United States amounted to about 2 per cent of US GNP.[4] But Eichengreen and Uzan later argued that despite its small size, the psychological impact of tangible US support did contribute to the restoration of market forces, the removal of shortages, and confidence in the future trajectory of Europe, which sustained investment programmes.[5] The OEEC did not turn out to be the seed bed of European integration, which came later through the European Coal and Steel Community, but it did bring European officials together to share information and screen requests for aid and later led to initiatives that reduced barriers to trade. Paradoxically, Milward later argued that the success of the Marshall Plan in perpetuating national priorities of full employment and growth reinforced nation states in Europe rather then diluting them.[6]

Figure 2.1 shows the relative position of a range of European countries by 1950 compared to 1938, and it is clear that German recovery lagged well behind other states in Europe.

Figure 2.2 shows the distribution of grants under the Marshall Plan scheme. The UK as America's closest ally was the largest recipient, followed by France. The Anglo-French strategy of co-operation at the outset appears to have paid off. West Germany, while the most needy of recipients, received only 10 per cent of grants and less than 5 per cent was given to regional rather than national programmes, so the strategy of retaining national identities in the programme also appears successful.

The size of Marshall Aid was clearly too small to resolve the global imbalance between the United States and the rest of the world on its own. Exchange controls had to be retained, but there was pressure to improve the functioning of international trade despite this obstacle. The outcome was a series of pragmatic regional or currency-based solutions to allow multilateralism among a limited range of countries while protecting against the dollar shortage. The first and largest of these groups was the Sterling Area, which comprised countries engaged in about half of the world's trade in the 1940s. This group of countries had traditionally pegged their exchange rates to sterling and so held the bulk of their reserves in sterling. They were mainly colonies or ex-colonies with the addition of some Middle Eastern

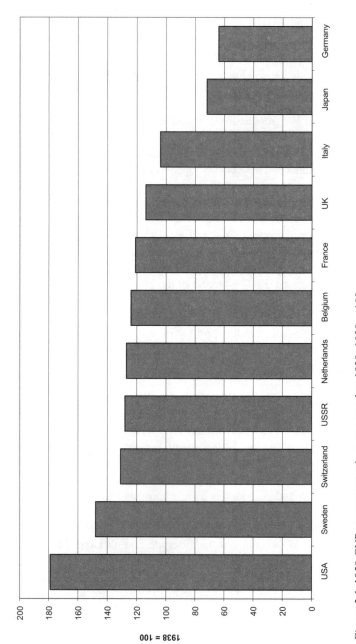

Figure 2.1 1950 GNP at constant prices compared to 1938: 1938 = 100.

Source: S. Pollard, *The International Economy since 1945*, Routledge, 1997

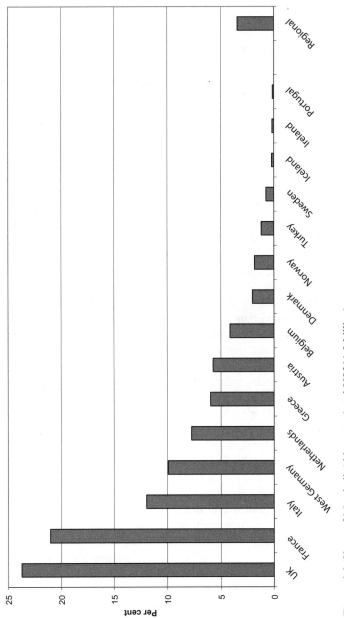

Figure 2.2 Share of Marshall Aid grants (total US$11.8 billion)

Source: Statistics and Reports Division, Agency for International Development, 1975

states and Iceland.[7] Many had accumulated large sterling assets during the war due to British expenditure in their territory and this increased their financial ties to the UK while also providing a source of conflict as they sought to liquidate these assets. The assets were held in the form of treasury bills or other British government securities and were thus a liability of the British government. Since they comprised four times the level of Britain's foreign exchange reserves, it was clearly impossible to allow the assets to be liquidated and converted immediately directly to other currencies. Even spending the funds on British production was hampered by scarcity of supply in Britain, and as a result a large proportion was blocked under a series of bilateral agreements with scheduled releases. From the late 1940s, the members of the Sterling Area traded more freely among themselves than with the rest of the world and retained tight exchange controls jointly against Europe and the United States while allowing freer payments within the Sterling Area. The Sterling Area persisted for twenty-eight years after the end of the war, being abandoned only in June 1972 when the sterling exchange rate floated and the government imposed controls on capital flows to the Sterling Area to bring them in line with other countries.

In 1949 a co-ordinated effort to correct the global imbalance was made by adjusting exchange rates against the US dollar. During the first half of 1949, the United States, the IMF and many European states were convinced that a significant depreciation of all European currencies against the US dollar would help to resolve what had clearly emerged as a fundamental disequilibrium. The Labour government in the UK was reluctant to use this method instead of the direct controls and planning to which they were committed. They expected inflation to eat up any adjustment in the nominal exchange rate and preferred to pursue nationalisation of industry and direct state control of resources to ensure they were used in the national interest. By the summer of 1949, however, international pressure was mounting and the decision was finally taken to devalue the pound on 18 September by 30 per cent, paving the way for other European and Sterling Area currencies also to devalue.

Even this readjustment was insufficient to encourage enough confidence for countries to free up their exchange controls and adhere to the requirements of the Articles of Agreement of the IMF. Along with the Sterling Area, another major regional monetary grouping was formed in 1950 to enhance multilateralism on a limited scale. By this time, the United States had abandoned its commitment to a globally based convertible currency system and helped to promote a European regional system of freer trade and payments even though this discriminated against the United States. In the five years since the Bretton Woods conference the US government had abandoned its opposition to discriminatory trade arrangements and also its commitment to a global multilateral trade and payments system. This was partly due to the lesson of Britain's disastrous experiment with convertibility in 1947, and also because of America's increasing emphasis on European economic integration as part of the strategy of creating a solid political as well as economic bulwark against communist expansion from Eastern Europe.

The EPU was founded in 1950 to allow a clearing system for European states, and it shared some characteristics with Keynes' abandoned ICU. The goal was to allow a country to offset a deficit with one partner using surpluses earned elsewhere in Europe without risking direct convertibility of currencies. The Bank for International Settlements held the accounts of the EPU, where surpluses and deficits of each country against all members as a whole were calculated monthly and expressed in EPU units of account (valued at the gold content of 1 US dollar). Each country was given a quota in the EPU equal to the value of 15 per cent of its trade in 1949 with other members. Countries were allowed to be in deficit over the short term up to 20 per cent of their quota, but as deficits accumulated they had to be settled increasingly in US dollars or gold. Surplus countries had to accept credit for the initial surpluses but could be paid in US dollars or gold as their balances accumulated. The United States contributed US$350 million to start the pool of credit, and there were eighteen initial members from Europe including Turkey and the UK. The terms of the EPU were reviewed on an annual basis, and gradually the threshold before settlement in US dollars or gold was reduced so that the system was 'hardened' or made closer to a convertible currency system. An important feature of the EPU was that it pledged members to reduce barriers to trade among themselves as part of the goal of increasing regional economic integration and increased growth. The EPU did not always operate smoothly and there were frequent tensions between persistent surplus and persistent deficit countries over the terms of settlement of these balances, but it contributed significantly to the overall growth in European trade during its period of operation from 1950–8.

The Cold War meant that international economic relations were divided along political lines. Countries of the Eastern Bloc were engaged in regional integration centred on the USSR and were excluded from Western trading systems by strategic embargoes. After rapid recovery in the 1950s, the benefits of this isolated grouping were quickly expiring by the end of the decade, and growth rates began to falter. The communist-led People's Republic of China, founded in 1949, was also excluded by trade embargoes, first from the United States in 1949 and then by members of the United Nations from 1950. Mao's strategy in the 1950s was to 'lean to one side' to attract investment and to trade with fellow communist states so that more than two-thirds of China's exports went to socialist countries, mainly Eastern

Europe and the USSR. However, a political rift in 1960 cut China off from relations with the USSR and its satellites. The disastrous Great Leap Forward of 1960–2 diverted resources from agriculture to industry, prompting a massive famine and economic crisis and was followed by a more moderate shift of Maoist policy to 'self-reliance' – that is, minimising dependence on international trade and investment and relying on national resources for industrial expansion. As in the USSR, this approach generated initial economic gains, but by the late 1960s these advances were eroded by exclusion from international trade, investment and technology, as well as by further domestic social and political disruption from the Cultural Revolution.

Conclusions and summary

This chapter has addressed a relatively short period, but these years were fundamental to determining the structure of the international economy over the next two decades. The priorities of freer trade on a multilateral basis were established and, while the original Bretton Woods institutions did not deliver their promise immediately, the process of their design had created a remarkable consensus about the direction (if not the pace) of reform. The emergence of the Cold War eroded the global approach that had been adopted during the war, but by 1950 regional solutions to international payments problems were already beginning to contribute to the period of sustained growth among developed nations that was to follow over the next two decades. The issues of developing nations had been raised through trade negotiations and also through the tensions over Britain's war obligations to the empire, but they had not been resolved and were pushed to the periphery of the building of the global economic architecture.

3   Years of growth 1950–73

From 1950 there were two decades of rapid growth in industrialised countries, driven by European economic integration and the liberalisation of international trade through the OEEC and GATT. Recovery from the war after 1950 was fairly swift, particularly in core industrial countries such as West Germany and the United States. The developed OECD group of countries grew by about 5.5 per cent p.a. during the 1950s and 1960s, while inflation remained moderate. In retrospect, this era was characterised as a prolonged period of prosperity and rising expectations that generated a range of social changes, including the feminist movement, environmentalism and the social protests associated with the 'hippy era'.

From 1945–51 Japan was occupied by the American military, where the economic mission had changed by 1947 from annihilating the military-industrial complex to rebuilding the industrial capacity of Japan in order to make it a powerful regional ally in the Cold War. As we have noted above, from the mid-1950s Japanese manufactures were highly competitive in global markets, so that Japan's share of world exports soared from 2 per cent in 1955 to 6 per cent by 1970. The Korean War of 1950–2 generated demand for Japanese production of vehicles and military supplies, which provided a crucial impetus to recovery and growth. Since the Americans spent US dollars in Japan, this allowed that country to avoid part of the dollar shortage that plagued the recovery of European states and also allowed Japanese industry to import state-of-the-art American technology, which helped launch Japan into two decades of high-speed growth. Demand for raw materials due to rearmament also spurred developing economies such as Malaysia (a major tin and rubber producer) and Western African states. High incomes spread industrialisation to a range of emerging markets in East Asia, such as South Korea and Taiwan, and allowed the diversification of economies such as Australia. The expansion of trade and incomes was accompanied by rapid growth in international capital flows, as American companies in particular spread their operations overseas and financial innovations such as the Eurodollar market emerged to meet the demands of customers for more sophisticated global financial services.

By the early 1960s, however, the Bretton Woods system was under persistent pressure as waning confidence in the core exchange rates of the US dollar and the pound sterling rocked the foundations of the pegged exchange rate system. The response was a series of ad hoc adjustments including the Gold Pool and swaps of short-term capital organised outside the IMF to sustain the system. The dominance of the Group of 10 wealthy countries (G10) in discussions on how to fundamentally reform the international economic system sidelined the IMF and eventually drove it to reassess its role.[1] In these decades the expansion of multinational companies and innovation in international financial markets seemed to challenge the influence of the state on economic outcomes. This was also the period when the needs of developing countries began to be recognised with the formation of the United Nations Conference on Trade and Development (UNCTAD) in 1964 and the launch of the 'development decade'. Despite these initiatives, the gap between rich and poor countries continued to grow, laying the seeds for crisis in the 1980s.

European integration: from the ECSC to the EEC

One of the most important drivers of economic growth during the two decades of prosperity in Western Europe from 1950 was the process of integration.[2] Falling barriers to economic exchange among a range of European states gave added impetus to the global trade initiatives discussed in the next section. The key fulcrum of the process was the geopolitical relationship between France and Germany; two countries that had been at the core of European military conflict since the nineteenth century. A final accommodation that would provide a lasting peace required some resolution between these two states. In the post-war settlement France was extremely conscious of the industrial powerhouse that had driven the German war machine and also of the importance of Germany's natural resources of coal, coke and steel for France's own industrial recovery. This reality prompted an ambitious and provocative proposal from France to share these critical resources on a European scale for the benefit of all European states.

Discussions between Jean Monnet (minister in charge of French reconstruction) and Robert Schuman (French foreign minister and previous finance minister) led to the genesis of the Schuman Plan in May 1950. Their vision was that the entire French and German production of coal and steel would be placed under a joint High Authority, which would then distribute the production. The organisation would be open to other Western European countries and would aim to create a common market in steel and coal to standardise prices and working and living conditions in the industry and to centralise and rationalise investment. After lengthy negotiation, the European Coal and Steel Community (ECSC) opened in April 1951, bringing together France, West Germany, Italy, the Netherlands, Belgium and Luxembourg. These countries subsequently became known as The Six as they steered the European integration project forward. The UK was notably absent, having rejected the invitation to join. The British government's unwillingness to devolve sovereignty to European institutions and the identification of Britain's economic priorities as lying outside Europe came to characterise the relationship between the UK and The Six during the 1950s, although this was to change early in the next decade. The British government was unwilling to cede sovereignty to a supranational institution and clung instead to relations with the commonwealth and the United States, although they did sign an Agreement of Association with the ECSC in 1954, giving them observer status.

The ECSC was undoubtedly a success and led quickly to plans to extend the model to all trade. The Dutch Foreign Minister Willem Beyen started planning for a more complete customs union in 1952 and found strongest support among the Belgians. A range of initiatives between 1952 and 1955 foundered, including a European Defence Community, before the Benelux states proposed a general common market in traded goods alongside collective action on energy and transport policy. The foreign ministers of The Six considered these proposals at a summit at Messina in May 1955 and delegated the details to a committee headed by Henri Spaak, the Belgian foreign minister.

There are four main types of economic integration:

1 Free trade area: members remove trade barriers against each other but are free to impose whatever tariffs they wish against the rest of the world.
2 Customs union: free internal trade among members and common external tariff.
3 Common market: free movement of factors of production (labour and capital) as well as goods.
4 Economic union: complete monetary and fiscal union entailing common domestic economic policies and greater centralised administration.

The plans for a free trade organisation based on the ECSC quickly became very ambitious and strayed into political spheres, including a European parliament as well as a customs union. At this point, in November 1955, the UK withdrew from the negotiations since aligning British tariffs with those of The Six would require the UK to abandon Imperial Preference and to impose tariffs on relatively inexpensive commonwealth food imports. The level of the common external tariff was also highly controversial among The Six, whose vision of the organisation ranged from a 'fortress' of protection (France) to a relatively open system (Belgium).

Finally, two treaties were drafted; one dealing with atomic energy and one with economic integration. They were signed in Rome on 25 March 1957 and the European Economic Community (EEC) and European Atomic Energy Community (Euratom) came into being on 1 January 1958. Through the EEC, the Treaty of Rome established the blueprint for a customs union among members with aspirations for a common market at some point in the future. The goal was to reduce the economic impact of political borders and create 'the foundations of an enduring and closer union among European peoples'. The progress of co-operation was not always smooth and deep conflicts periodically split members, but the EEC proved resilient to these tensions and continued to evolve throughout the 1960s. Free internal trade and a common external tariff was achieved in stages by July 1968.

An important impetus for co-operation was to defend the agricultural sectors of the member states, in particular for France, and so a common market for agricultural products along the lines of the ECSC with common prices was discussed as early as 1959. Finally, in January 1962 the principles for a common agricultural policy (CAP) were adopted whereby all European farmers would receive the same price for their produce, which was set centrally to ensure sustainable livelihoods. High prices of output for farmers encouraged them to increase production beyond what the European market could sustain even when cheaper imports were excluded by tariffs. This resulted in expensive accumulations of surplus agricultural produce, and finally the CAP began to pay farmers not to plant their fields in order to restrain production. The outcome was that the CAP was the most costly aspect of the EEC budget and became controversial for increasing consumer prices for food. Politically, the CAP was also a source of tension. In July 1965, France (although a keen supporter of the CAP) broke off negotiations on the financial aspects of the programme and withdrew its representatives from the European Council for seven months in what was termed the 'empty chair crisis'. Later in the 1960s as European exchange rates became unstable, it was required that farmers be compensated for the changes in local prices arising from depreciation or revaluation. These so-called compensatory payments soon added considerably to the financial burden of the CAP and encouraged the regional impetus toward stable exchange rates within the EEC and, ultimately, monetary union.

Despite these challenges, the success of the EEC in generating growth in trade and incomes attracted other countries to join, although no candidates were successful until the UK, Ireland and Denmark joined in 1973. In the meantime, the UK continued its preferential trade relations with the Sterling Area group of countries and also joined six other European countries outside the EEC in creating the European Free Trade Area for manufactures in 1960. A year later the UK, Ireland and Denmark applied to join the EEC, but they were excluded for the next ten years. Some members, particularly France, worried that expansion threatened the cohesive character of the EEC and would hamper progress on agriculture and monetary union. Bringing the UK with its close commonwealth economic ties into the system was particularly problematic. The EEC did, however, reach out to former colonies of its members, particularly in Africa, signing the Yaounde Convention with seventeen African states and Madagascar to reduce barriers to trade in July 1963.

Trade liberalisation, market integration and economic growth

As noted in Chapter 2, after the war, policy-makers put great emphasis on the capacity for reduced trade barriers to promote global economic growth. The EEC achieved this process for European countries, but there were also other forums in which tariffs and other barriers on trade were reduced. The most important was the GATT, which grew from its humble beginnings to be the key framework for global trade negotiations until 1995. Table 3.1 shows the outcome of the series of negotiating 'rounds' in the 1960s, culminating in the Kennedy Round of 1964–7. Reducing trade protection was a difficult policy for governments to pursue since the interests of domestic producers could be threatened by increased competition from foreign production. The success of the Kennedy Round was partly due to the 1962 Trade Expansion Act, whereby the US Congress delegated greater

Table 3.1 Impact of the GATT

Tariff round	Year	Number of concessions	Total trade affected	Average depth of tariff cuts (%)
Geneva	1947	45,000	US$10 billion	19
Annecy	1949	5,000		2
Torquay	1950–1	8,700		3
Geneva	1955–6	2,700		2
Dillon	1960–2	4,400	US$25 billion	7
Kennedy	1964–7	8,159	US$49 billion	35
Tokyo	1973–9			33

Source: W. Asbeek-Brusse, *Tariffs, Trade and European Integration, 1947–1957; from Study Group to Common Market*, St Martin's Press, 1997, p. 118. Tokyo data from WTO website.

negotiating powers to the US President in an effort to reduce the power of domestic political opposition to reducing tariffs.

The integration of markets and the efficiency of trade were enhanced by the introduction of currency convertibility for trade among most countries at the end of 1958, and also by the expansion of multinational corporations, particularly from the United States. By 1970 the United States accounted for about half of the world's foreign direct investment, with European companies taking up a further 37.5 per cent. Canada was the largest single host for American companies, given the close affinity between these markets combined with Canadian trade barriers against US goods. In the 1960s MNCs overwhelmingly came from developed nations and were located in other industrialised countries. This form of expansion was encouraged by the ease and speed of travel and communications, strong business confidence and growing incomes in Europe. The cost of passenger air travel fell by about half from 1950 to 1970 in constant dollars, while the average price of a three-minute call from New York to London fell from 53 cents to 32 cents.[3] American companies that had exhausted the economies of scale of production in their home markets sought to exploit their technological advantages and marketing and managerial expertise to capture new markets. By the 1970s, more FDI was directed to developing regions such as Latin America to exploit natural resources and cheaper labour as wage costs in the United States and Europe rose.

Persistent inequalities

Trade and payments liberalisation, the spread of industrial innovation and rises in labour productivity all contributed to rapid and sustained rates of growth in most developed countries during the twenty years from 1950. This period is sometimes called the 'golden age' or the 'long boom', but this experience was not shared by all nations. Indeed, during these decades inequality among nations increased rather than decreased as rich nations' growth outstripped that of poorer economies.

We have seen that in the 1940s and 1950s the US government devoted considerable political and monetary resources to restoring the war-torn economies of Western Europe as a bulwark against communism, and this strategy was remarkably successful. The Communist Revolution in China from 1947–9 and the Korean War of 1950–2, as the first 'hot' conflicts of the Cold War, highlighted the importance of political and economic stability in poorer nations to the success of capitalism as the dominant global system. The US launched substantial aid programmes for South Korea and the Republic of China (Taiwan) to counter the influence of the People's Republic of China (PRC), and these helped in the transition to industrial recovery in these two countries. In the 1950s they developed their labour-intensive industries behind protective trade barriers, but the gains from import substitution were waning by the end of the decade. During the 1960s, partly under American liberal pressure, these states embarked on ambitious development programmes based on attracting foreign capital and penetrating the international market for a range of labour-intensive manufactures in the case of Taiwan and, increasingly, heavy industry in South Korea. The success of this export-orientated strategy outstripped most expectations, with annual growth in GDP in the 1960s averaging about 9 per cent in each case.[4]

The commitment to promoting the growth of incomes in less developed countries was recognised not only as a strategic but also as a humanitarian priority. In the process, developing countries themselves seized the initiative in lobbying for their interests, particularly as many colonies of European empires gained constitutional independence in the late 1950s, including Nigeria, Ghana and Malaysia. In 1961 the United Nations launched the UN Development Decade, and US President John F. Kennedy promoted an Alliance for Progress to bring together the interests of North and South America. The politicisation of the issue of development and its domination by Cold War interests led to the first Non-aligned Conference on Problems of Economic Development in Cairo in 1962, as poorer countries sought to leverage their strategic importance to gain economic support. This initiative culminated in the formation of UNCTAD in 1964.

Despite apparent progress in recognising the importance of global economic development, and the successful industrialisation and rapid growth of some states in East Asia such as Japan, South Korea and Taiwan, the gap between rich and poor nations widened rather than shrank during the 1960s. Table 3.2 shows the GDP per capita for poorer countries relative to that of the high income OECD economies. In 1960, low and middle income economies' GDP per capita was about 10 per cent that of the OECD, but by 1970 this had fallen to 8 per cent. Particular areas such as Latin America fell behind during the 1960s, falling from 24 per cent of OECD GDP per capita in 1960 to 20 per cent by 1970. Overall, the share of developing countries in world trade also contracted from 27 per cent of world exports in 1955 to 19 per cent in 1970. The intractable problem of economic development for poorer nations was clearly established as poverty, undernourishment and economic dependence continued and worsened for many states. In retrospect, the evidence suggests that those countries that engaged most vigorously with the expansion of international trade in manufactures and flows of capital grew faster than those that opted out of the international system by erecting barriers to trade and payments, or those who were plagued by domestic political and military disturbance. On this weak foundation, the following decade was extraordinarily difficult as the global

Table 3.2 Ratio of GDP per capita to high income OECD average (nominal current US$)

	1960	1965	1970	1975	1980
Low and middle income countries	0.10	0.09	0.08	0.08	0.07
Least developed countries (UN classification)	N/A	0.06	0.05	0.05	0.03
World average	0.30	0.29	0.27	0.26	0.25
Sub-Saharan Africa	0.09	0.08	0.08	0.08	0.07
Latin America and Caribbean	0.24	0.22	0.20	0.21	0.21

Source: World Bank, *World Development Indicators*

system was shaken by a series of shocks that halted and even reversed economic development in both rich and poor countries.

Challenges to the pegged exchange rate system

Once most currencies were convertible for trade purposes from the end of 1958, the international monetary system finally began to operate along the rules laid out at Bretton Woods: a pegged exchange rate system based on stable rates to the US dollar. Almost immediately, however, cracks in the system began to appear. As noted in Chapter 1, the Mundell-Fleming Trilemma suggests that with a pegged exchange rate, countries have to maintain controls on international capital flows in order to pursue independent economic policies. Otherwise an expansionist policy will generate inflation and then speculation about whether the pegged rate is sustainable. Controls on capital flows will prevent such a sentiment from pushing the exchange rate off its peg and so allow greater policy independence. From the 1940s there was a consensus that trade was good for growth, but on the other hand there existed a general suspicion of flows of short-term capital such as those that had destabilised the global economy in the 1930s. This was how the Bretton Woods system was conceived; pegged exchange rates to ensure co-operation and stability, tight controls on capital flows to allow policy sovereignty, combined with more liberal trade in goods to promote growth.

From the 1960s controls on international investment and other capital flows became much more difficult to enforce. The prevalence of currency convertibility for trade purposes meant that it was more difficult to police capital controls. Financial innovation also accelerated due to the demand for international finance to meet the needs of the swelling numbers of

MNCs and others who required services to finance the growing volume of international economic transactions. The most important innovation was the Eurodollar market in London at the end of the 1950s. Through this market, companies, governments and individuals could make US dollar-denominated deposits at banks in London, which then lent these funds on to borrowers anywhere in the world. There were limits on the interest rates payable on sterling deposits in the UK and on US dollar deposits in the United States, which left a market gap for banks in London to offer higher interest rates for dollar deposits in London. This attracted funds from Eastern European states that wanted to use the US dollar but feared that their deposits might be confiscated if they were located in the United States. Several central banks and many US companies operating in Europe also found the rates in London attractive and the value of Eurodollar deposits grew quickly. Banks could switch these funds to sterling for local investment or loan the dollars on to third parties. From 1963, companies and governments began to issue dollar denominated bonds in the City of London and created a market known as the Eurobond market. The outcome was large flows of short-term capital that were not subject to national regulation: so-called offshore markets. With uncontrolled flows of capital, states soon found that it was more and more difficult to sustain pegged exchange rates in the wake of adverse market sentiment.

A further pressure on the system was the so-called 'Triffin Paradox'. Most countries pegged their currencies to either the US dollar or the pound sterling and these currencies were the two main international reserve assets. As the international economy grew, there was an increasing demand for foreign exchange reserves to act as working balances for a larger volume of transactions and also to intervene in foreign exchange markets to protect pegged exchange rates. Since reserve assets were issued by nation-states, an increase in global reserves meant that the US and the UK were selling more government securities overseas to supply the necessary global liquidity. While the value of sterling held in overseas reserves was fairly constant from the 1950s to the 1970s, the amount of US dollar assets in the international economy soared. As the volume of US dollars increased much faster than the amount of gold, it was clear that all US dollars would not be redeemable at the rate of US$35 per ounce if they were all presented for conversion at once. Confidence in the fixed gold value of the US dollar eroded. This prompted some countries, such as France, to try to accumulate gold reserves by selling off their US dollars, putting further pressure on the US dollar's gold value.

From the early 1960s it was clear that the system could become unsustainable and plans began for replacing national currencies as reserve assets. These talks focused first in the IMF and then among the G10 group of advanced industrialised countries who took leadership of the international monetary system. In the end, the negotiations were very prolonged and did not arrive at a final solution. The United States worried that replacing the US dollar would make it more costly to finance its deficits, and it did not want a run on the US dollar to prompt a break with gold. France and some other European countries, on the other hand, felt that the ability to issue an international reserve asset gave the US an 'exorbitant privilege' since other countries were obliged to accept US Treasury Bills and other government debt as reserves. While the United States was running substantial balance-of-payments deficits, American multinationals were buying assets in other countries, mainly in Europe. In this sense, countries in surplus that accumulated US debt were financing the overseas expansion of US corporations. Other important criticisms were that the system helped the US finance an unpopular war in Vietnam and pursue an unsustainable expansionist policy at home. In order to maintain the pegged exchange rates once capital flows were more free, countries had to follow movements in the US interest rate. German politicians were highly critical of the inflationary pressure that this put on their economy and wanted the US to correct its balance-of-payments deficit.

From being the main surplus country when the Bretton Woods system had been designed, the United States had become a major debtor, although it remained the richest and biggest economy in the world. The US economy moved from a trade surplus of US$1–2 billion in the mid-1960s to a $1–2 billion deficit in the early 1970s as export competitiveness eroded. As relative American productivity declined compared to Europe and Japan, the US dollar became increasingly overvalued – that is, the official price did not reflect demand and supply in the market. In 1963 the Kennedy administration imposed controls on outward flows of capital, including a tax on interest on foreign lending, to try to reduce balance-of-payments deficits, but this did not prove sufficient. The pressure was exacerbated by the inflationary effects of the Johnson administration's Great Society programme and expenditure on the Vietnam War. Further controls on outward flows of capital in 1965 curtailed the ability of US MNCs to borrow in the United States and for American banks to lend overseas. Still, the deficit grew and the core of the Bretton Woods system seemed fatally flawed.

While negotiations on reforming the entire system progressed, a series of interim measures propped up the system. In 1960 the central banks of the main advanced industrialised countries formed the Gold Pool to keep the price of gold from rising in the private market.[5] They intervened in the gold market to retain the Bretton Woods value of US$35 per ounce until March 1968 when speculative pressures made this unsustainable. In 1961 the same central banks began to organise swaps of short-term credit among themselves to help when market pressure threatened exchange rate stability. In addition, the resources of the IMF were increased through rises in the quotas contributed by all states. In 1959 there was a 50 per cent increase, in 1966 a further 25 per cent and in 1970 another 30 per cent, so that the funds available through the IMF grew from US$9.2 billion in 1958 to $21.3 billion in 1970. Many countries used these facilities during the 1960s, including the UK, Italy and France. The IMF resources were further enhanced in 1964 when the world's ten richest countries pledged to lend to the IMF in case of very large borrowings from the Fund. This General Agreement to Borrow identified what became known as the G10 group of countries. To prevent the wholesale selling off of foreign exchange reserves held in sterling, in September 1968 the UK offered to guarantee the US dollar value of 90 per cent of the sterling reserves held by thirty-four countries in return for a pledge from these countries to hold a minimum proportion of their reserves in sterling. This effort to avoid a wholesale diversification of reserves away from the pound, which would have prompted a disastrous collapse in sterling, was underpinned by a US$2 billion line of credit from the G10 countries in what was known as the Basel Agreement. This, and subsequent support schemes, resolved the problem of sterling's reserve currency status, but the US dollar was still at risk.

The outcome of the prolonged and often ill-tempered discussions among the G10 and the IMF over how to fix the pegged exchange rate system was the Special Drawing Right (SDR), which was finally agreed in 1967. The SDR was originally meant to be a reserve asset that could be deliberately issued and distributed by the IMF to supplement the use of the US dollar as reserve asset. It had a fixed value in terms of gold that was the same as the US dollar (1/35 of a troy ounce) and each participating member was given SDRs in proportion to their quota in IMF. The idea was to scientifically and deliberately expand international liquidity in line with growth of world trade (sharing some characteristics with Keynes' Bancor from the ICU). Altogether SDR9.3 billion was distributed in stages from 1970–2 (about 6 per cent of global reserves), and a further SDR12.1 billion in total from 1979–81 (bringing SDRs back to close to 6 per cent of global reserves, which had grown in the meantime). But the SDR never lived up to its expectations as an alternative reserve asset since further distributions were stymied by disagreement over the appropriate allocation. As global foreign exchange reserves grew, the share of SDR gradually fell to below 1 per cent by 2003 (according to IMF figures). The US dollar remained the primary global reserve asset, although in the 2000s the euro began to increase its presence, as we shall see in Chapter 6.

The power and influence of the G10 outside the IMF prompted concern among developing and other countries that their interests would be sacrificed to those of the world's richest nations. The IMF sought to protect the interests of a broader range of countries, but the economic and political power of the G10 was overwhelming. The reform discussions only returned to the IMF once the G10 talks had come to an impasse. Indeed, expanding the forum for discussion to a broader and more disparate group of countries was one way to slow down and dilute the prospects for radical change. After the SDR was created it was clear that this would not be a lasting solution and in 1972 a much wider constituency of representatives of twenty states making up the Committee on Reform of the International Monetary System took up the negotiations. These discussions quickly became so diffuse and complex that there was no tangible outcome, although their report in 1974 did bring a wide range of developed and developing states into closer contact with the global policy-making context than had been the case before. This episode was a precursor to ongoing problems over the representativeness of the governance of the international economy through such institutions as the IMF that led to the foundation of the Group of 20 (G20) in 1999.

Collapse of the international monetary system 1971–3

The Bretton Woods system finally collapsed at the end of a series of shuddering crises. From the early 1960s there was a series of readjustments of European currencies to take account of the productivity of the West German economy vis-à-vis other European states. In November 1967 the UK Labour government finally allowed sterling to be devalued by 14.3 per cent from its 1949 level. This had been resisted not only by successive British governments (who feared inflationary pressure at home) but also by the American administration, which viewed a stable pound as a bulwark against speculative pressure on the US dollar. During the 1960s, the vulnerability of the entire international monetary system to a collapse of sterling allowed the UK to contract repeated rounds of financial support to protect the sterling exchange rate. The prediction that a devaluation of the pound would generate systemic instability appeared justified as the market anticipated a depreciation of the US dollar in early 1968 and there was a rush to exchange dollars to gold, culminating in a frenzy of gold purchases in March 1968. From September 1967 to March 1968 supporting the gold price in London cost the Gold Pool US$3.5 billion. This was deemed insupportable and from this date a two-tiered market emerged: a private market at a rate set by demand and supply, and an official market used by central banks that operated at the rate of US$35 per ounce. In May 1968 a rash of student protests and political instability spread across Western Europe, particularly in France where the de Gaulle government was brought down and wages soared. This added to the fragility of the exchange rate system as the franc was devalued in August 1969 (by 11 per cent) and West Germany resisted pressure to revalue the Deutschmark until October 1969 (by 10 per cent).

At the centre of the system, the American economy was also rocked by a series of crises. From 1968–9 the balance of trade worsened due to domestic price inflation. This prompted the Federal Reserve (the US central bank) to raise interest rates (inter-bank overnight lending rates) from 4 per cent in October 1967 to 6 per cent in mid-1968 and then to 9.2 per cent in October 1969. Higher rates in New York prompted an inflow of short-term capital, particularly from Europe. By the end of 1969 it appeared that the monetary stringency had over-shot its target and a recession loomed. GDP growth fell from 4.1 per cent in 1968 to 2.4 per cent in 1969, and so in 1970 interest rates were lowered again. This in turn prompted a huge short-term capital outflow of US$6.5 billion in 1970, soaring to $20 billion in 1971 and contributing to a US balance-of-payments deficit of $30 billion in that year. This flood of US dollars into the international monetary system made the pegged rate system based on a fixed gold value of the US dollar unsustainable.

When Bretton Woods had been designed, the United States was the main creditor country and the onus of adjustment was placed on deficit countries to correct imbalances. By 1971 the most powerful country in the world was a deficit country and this changed the pattern of influence in the system. With its political as well as strategic power and economic wealth, the United States could still wield considerable influence to force other countries to act in America's interests. In 1969 the Republican Richard Nixon had gained the presidency and with his Treasury Secretary John Connolly developed a more nationalistic posture with regard to international economic relations. Connolly famously remarked that 'foreigners are out to screw us. Our job is to screw them first'. In the wake of the global scramble out of US dollars, in August 1971 Nixon announced a unilateral challenge to the rest of the world. Although Nixon had been considering some kind of démarche for months, the final plan was devised hastily at Camp David with Connolly and announced on television on the evening of Sunday, 15 August. There were three elements: suspending sales of gold by the US Treasury so that the dollar was no longer convertible to gold, a surcharge to increase the cost of imports by 10 per cent and cuts in US aid programmes. In addition, a variety of domestic policies were announced, including a wage/price freeze and fiscal cuts. The speech was clearly directed at other countries as Nixon demanded the removal of specific trade barriers against US goods, that Europe should contribute more to its own defence costs in the Cold War and that other countries should realign exchange rates to help to reduce the American deficit. Essentially, Nixon was threatening protectionism and a trade war unless other countries contributed to reducing the US deficit. The burden of adjustment was to be shifted firmly from the United States as debtor to the creditors.

The Nixon Shock, as it became known, prompted a panicked response in the rest of the world. In September 1971 the finance ministers of the G10 countries and the governors of their central banks met in London to decide how to go forward and avoid the reversal of the hard-fought trade liberalisation that had been achieved since 1945. A main axis of conflict was between France, which wanted a return to the gold standard, and the Americans, who sought adjustment in exchange rates by other countries to take the pressure off the US dollar. Initially nobody questioned the need to return to a pegged exchange rate system, albeit at different parities. Academic opinion was beginning to recognise the benefits of more flexible exchange rates for economic freedom in an environment of open capital markets, but politicians and central bankers were loath to remove the anchor of exchange rate stability. Some in the US Treasury advocated floating or flexible rates, but this was hotly resisted in Europe, where the transaction costs of exchange rate instability within the EEC were clearly apparent, especially through the CAP. Eventually a compromise was reached at a series of bilateral meetings in the Azores on 13–14 December 1971 between President Nixon and President Pompidou of France. The deal was ratified by the G10 in Washington on 17–18 December 1971 in what came to be known as the Smithsonian Agreement. Essentially, the US had got its way and other countries adjusted their exchange rates substantially to offset part of the loss of American competitiveness. The gold value of the US dollar was increased from $35 to $38 per ounce (although the US dollar was no longer convertible to gold) and the 10 per cent import surcharge was lifted. In return, other currencies re-pegged to the US dollar within wider boundaries of ±2.25 per cent instead of ±1 per cent to allow greater independence from US policy.

One of the outcomes of this debacle was the recognition of the importance of Japan to international economic relations. Japan's share of global exports had tripled from 2 per cent to 6 per cent from 1955 to 1970, exceeding the share of Canada (according to UNCTAD figures), and its manufacturers had been highly successful in penetrating US and European markets. Japanese officials had usually sat on the sidelines of G10 meetings, but the dramatic growth of the Japanese economy, helped by the increasingly undervalued yen exchange rate (which had been set in 1949 and remained unchanged for over twenty years), meant that Japan was central to the reform of the pegged rate system. Initially reluctant to revalue its currency as much as the Americans demanded, eventually Japan agreed to the largest revaluation of all the G10 states. From the 1970s the bilateral trade balance of Japan and the United States became a cornerstone of global trade relations as the US sought to remedy the rising flood of relatively inexpensive and high quality Japanese products into American households.

A second important development arising from the Nixon Shock was that the debate over exchange rate realignment and the introduction of wider bands of flexibility focused European policy-makers on their own distinctive priorities. The integration project to which Europe was committed and from which they had already benefited so much depended on exchange rate stability. With open economies, the transaction costs of fluctuating rates were much higher among members of the EEC than was true for the rest of the world. The compensation due under the CAP to farmers each time there was a realignment of European currencies was a further impetus to retain stable rates. From 1969, therefore, the EEC members had begun to follow their own path to greater monetary co-ordination. The Hague Summit pledged the members to plan for economic and monetary union, and in March 1972 The Six took positive steps toward monetary union by pegging their exchange rates to each other with boundaries of 1.125 per cent above and below parity while fluctuating against the US dollar at margins of ±2.25 per cent. This became known as the European Snake (denoting the horizontal linking of their currencies) in the Tunnel (the margin of 'wiggle' against the US dollar and the rest of the world's currencies).

Although much lauded at the time, the Smithsonian Agreement was in the end short-lived. The parities did not command the confidence of the market and speculation began almost immediately. Freer capital flows combined with the lack of commitment to common economic policies meant that the pegged exchange rate system was under considerable pressure. At the beginning of 1973 a speculative run on the US dollar began and Japan abandoned its parity on 10 February. Two days later representatives from the G10 met and agreed to devalue the US dollar to $42.2/oz and the pound, lira, Swiss franc and Canadian dollar all began to float. By 1 March the crisis had peaked and international currency markets in the US were closed until 19 March, by which time most currencies were floating. The European Snake 'came out of the Tunnel': its member currencies remained pegged to each other but floated against the US dollar from 16 March 1973. The Bretton Woods pegged exchange rate regime was dead, although this was not formally acknowledged by the IMF until 1976, when the IMF agreed to accept the legitimacy of permanently floating exchange rate regimes.

Conclusions and summary

After the dramatic conclusion of the Bretton Woods meeting in 1944, recognition of the limitations to international economic co-operation posed by an increasingly politically divided global system led to regional and partial solutions to international payments liberalisation. More firm progress was made on the commitment to freer trade through the EEC, the GATT and the OECD so that the world economy recovered and then grew quickly, although the benefits were distributed unevenly. The imbalance between industrial and developing economies was soon revealed as the period of sustained post-war growth ended abruptly in the early 1970s.

4 Years of crisis 1973–85

During the 1970s the international economy was rocked by the collapse of the international monetary system and by successive oil crises. The days when sustained economic growth each year was taken for granted were over and new challenges of unemployment, recession and inflation undermined the cohesion of the international economy. This chapter begins with the commodity and oil price booms and their impact on international economic relations. The combination of inflation and slow growth made it difficult to implement the traditional Keynesian economic tools to stabilise the economy and prompted a shift in economic ideology that favoured freer market forces. Efforts to co-ordinate the supervision of the rapidly growing and increasingly complex international financial markets also failed. By the early 1980s, the problems of unequal growth revealed themselves in a sovereign debt crisis that threatened the foundation of the financial system of industrialised countries and drew the IMF back to the centre of global policy-making.

OPEC and the oil crisis

With many governments freed from the constraints of the pegged exchange rate system in the early 1970s, faster growth became an easier policy target for the core industrialised countries. This expansionism was further encouraged by the rapid increase in the global money supply, largely the result of sustained US balance-of-payments deficits through the end of the 1960s and the beginning of 1970s. From March 1973 the US dollar became cheaper against European currencies as President Nixon allowed the exchange rate to sink. Surging demand in rapidly growing industrial economies for food and for raw materials for construction pushed up the revenues of many primary product-producing countries that still pegged their exchange rates to the US dollar. The combination of large surpluses and a depreciating currency led to strong inflationary pressure for many countries such as Malaysia, Australia and New Zealand. Other countries, such as India as well as parts of Africa and Asia, suffered from drought and poor harvests that inflated the price of food, further adding to inflation. In this volatile environment with fluctuating exchange rates, a commodity market boom and inflation, the first oil crisis struck global markets in the autumn of 1973.

Although triggered by a political event, there were several economic bases of the 1973 oil crisis. First, international demand for oil is price inelastic, which is another way of saying that the demand for oil is not as responsive to changes in price as some other goods. This is partly because moving to substitutes such as coal or nuclear energy tends to be costly since entrenched technology makes it expensive to switch from one source of energy to another. In the 1960s, industry, automobiles, home heating and electricity had come to rely on relatively cheap oil as the main source of energy. Large price rises would tend to increase producer revenue rather than decrease demand dramatically – that is, international demand was not very sensitive to rises in price. Second, the supply of oil was fairly concentrated geographically in OPEC. Figure 4.1 shows that OPEC's share rose from 40 per cent of world crude oil production in 1960 to peak at 55 per cent in 1973. Saudi Arabia and small emirates around the Persian Gulf produced 17 per cent of the world's oil. Algeria, Iran, Iraq and Venezuela together produced 22 per cent, while Indonesia and Nigeria produced 6 per cent. By 1985, OPEC's share had fallen below 30 per cent as other supplies in the US and UK were exploited. This geographic concentration meant that the potential for monopoly profits was strong if supply could be controlled by the OPEC members.

As Figure 4.2 shows, oil prices had been rising from the early 1970s due to increased demand from growing industrial economies (from US$1.80 per barrel at the start of 1970 to $2.60 at the start of 1973). In October 1973, Western political support for Israel in the Arab-Israeli war triggered a co-ordinated supply embargo by Middle Eastern states against the United States and other countries. The OPEC embargo on sales to industrial countries was soon replaced by deliberate price rises, enforced by a restriction of supply. This strategy was immediately effective, and by December 1973 the price of crude oil had doubled over the October level. From early 1973 to early 1974 the US dollar price of imported crude oil more than tripled from $3 to $10 per barrel. Such a sharp rise had a devastating impact on international economic relations as well as on consumers and producers.

The impact of the oil crisis was felt in three main ways. First, as more income was spent on oil for electricity, home heating or other oil-intensive industries, less was available to be spent on consumption of other goods, which then suffered from declining demand. This is known as the substitution effect, which spread recession from oil-intensive sectors to the rest

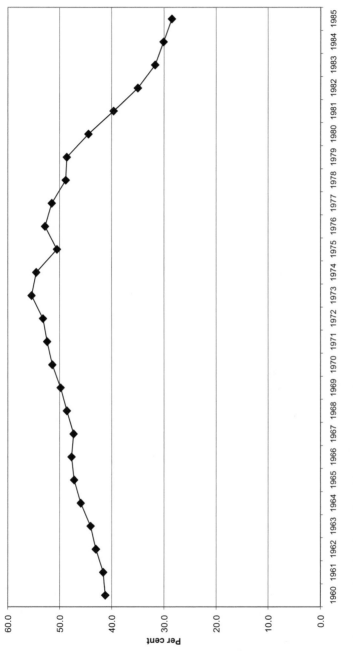

Figure 4.1 OPEC's share of world crude oil production 1960–85 (%)

Source: OPEC.org

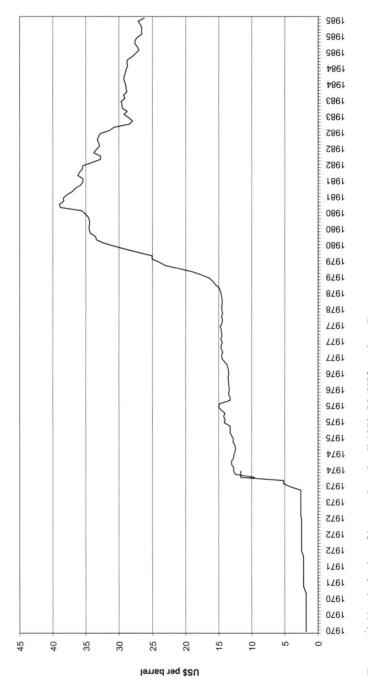

Figure 4.2 Nominal price of imported crude oil 1970–85 (US$ per barrel)

Source: US Energy Information Administration, www.eia.doe.gov/emeu/steo/pub/fsheets/petroleumprices.xls

of the economy. Second, wages are usually the largest cost in production but they tend to be inflexible in a downward direction since workers resist nominal cuts in pay, particularly in an inflationary environment. When industry cannot offset increases in the cost of oil input by cutting wages, they cut jobs instead. The result is a fall in employment and falling production rather than reductions in wages and costs. Finally, because post-war technologies had relied on a high oil content of manufactured goods, as costs rose these were passed on to the consumer and so general inflation increased. Together, these three forces delivered inflation, unemployment and slow growth.

The oil crisis also had implications for international economic relations as a substantial global imbalance emerged between oil exporters and oil importers. Importers of oil were faced with large trade deficits while OPEC countries accumulated large surpluses. Ideally, when one set of countries increases its exports, it spends the proceeds on imported goods from or investments in the countries to which it exports. In this case, the export surplus is 'recycled' back into the international economy and there is no sustained imbalance. In the case of the oil crisis, however, the OPEC surpluses were not easily spent on imports and so reserves were not redistributed through trade. A lot of the profits comprised royalties paid by oil companies directly to governments and were not distributed to the population, so they tended to accumulate in sovereign reserves rather than being spent on consumption. This effect was reinforced by the uneven distribution of income in many oil producing states where relatively few people controlled the bulk of the proceeds and most of the population did not reap the benefits. These factors prolonged the imbalance between surplus and deficit countries.

Table 4.1 shows Argy's estimates of how OPEC's surplus in 1974 was allocated. About 20 per cent was invested in American assets and 13 per cent in the UK, including equities and property. Very little was loaned

Table 4.1 Disbursement of OPEC surplus 1974 (US$ billion)

Total financial surplus	*55.0*
Invested in the United States	11.1
Eurocurrency deposits	22.8
International organisations	4.0
Loans to developing countries	2.5
Invested in UK	7.2
Other loans	4.5
Other investments	3.0

Source: V. Argy, *The Postwar International Money Crisis*, Allen & Unwin, 1981

directly to developing economies and the largest share (over 40 per cent) was deposited in European banks in the form of Eurocurrency deposits.

The immediate impact of the oil price increase on individual countries was determined partly by the degree of dependence on imported oil and partly by the flexibility of the national economy. Oil dependence was relatively low in West Germany, where oil met only 55 per cent of energy requirements, compared with Japan, which met 75 per cent of its energy needs through imported oil. However, Japan's economy and industrial organisation proved more flexible, and it was able to adapt more quickly to the new environment than many European and American economies. Poor countries trying to embark on industrialisation were especially hard hit as they had few reserves to draw upon, and this sowed the seeds of the third world debt crisis a decade later. In the short term, most governments sought to contain inflationary pressure through higher interest rates and cuts in government spending, which undermined growth. The new, more flexible exchange rate system did ease the pressure on deficit countries since they could let their exchange rate bear the burden to some degree by devaluing their currency.

By first half of 1974 a major global recession was underway, described as the worst downturn since the 1930s depression. Unlike the 1930s, when output and prices were both falling rapidly, this time as growth slowed inflation continued to gather pace. This faced policy-makers with a new dilemma that their Keynesian ideological foundations could not resolve. Rather than a trade-off between inflation and unemployment, states were faced with both problems simultaneously. This phenomenon became known by the ugly short-hand term 'stagflation', representing stagnating growth combined with inflation. If prices are rising too fast, the Keynesian response was to constrain consumer and producer demand through high interest rates and cuts in government spending or tax increases. But these contractionary policies also have the effect of reducing production and employment and thus reinforcing the downturn in growth. Initially, many governments tried to sustain economic activity through expansionary policies, but by the mid-1970s most countries tended to target the inflationary consequences of the crisis in the hope that once this was under control, growth could resume. In 1974–5 industrial production in OECD countries fell about 11 per cent on average (13 per cent in the US). Unemployment peaked at 8.5 per cent in the United States in 1975, which was almost twice as high as the average of the previous decade (although less than the 10 per cent levels of 2010). Even in Japan, where reported unemployment rates were exceedingly low, the rate of unemployment passed 2 per cent in 1976, which was twice the rate at the start of the decade.

The impact was also felt on international trade as countries sought to conserve foreign exchange for essential oil imports and avoided spending on other goods. Nevertheless, the Tokyo Round of GATT was launched in 1973 and involved 102 countries, up from sixty-two in the previous Kennedy Round of 1964–7. The nine major industrial participants cut their average tariff rates by one third, bringing tariffs on industrial products down from 7 per cent to an average of 4.7 per cent. These reductions primarily benefited rich countries since most industrial product trade was among rich nations. Efforts to extend agreements to non-tariff barriers and to reduce farm protection were less successful, leaving primary product producers still at a disadvantage in terms of competing with the protected food and raw material sectors of rich countries such as Japan, the EEC and the United States.

While industrialised countries were able to float their currencies, slow down their (previously relatively rapid) economic growth and use up reserves to cushion the impact of the crisis, developing nations were forced to rely on international borrowing to fund their trade deficits. As we shall see in the next section, this response was ultimately unsustainable, but at the time it was promoted by the IMF and other agencies, which interpreted the recycling of OPEC surpluses to less developed countries through international capital markets as a sign that the international economic system could and would re-balance itself through market forces. The IMF also arranged an Oil Facility to provide extra liquidity for deficit countries funded by OPEC. From 1974–8 the real price of oil was relatively constant compared to the prices of manufactured goods, and recovery began for most countries from 1976. The optimistic predictions that the crisis would recede, however, were soon dashed by the onset of another oil price shock.

The second oil crisis was also prompted by political conflict, this time by the Iranian Revolution at the beginning of 1979, which reduced that country's supply of oil and increased prices by about 170 per cent from the end of 1978 to the first quarter of 1981. The current account surplus of oil producers escalated from US$3 billion in 1978 to $115 billion in 1980, while the current account deficits of non-oil developing economies ballooned from $39 billion in 1978 to $100 billion in 1982. Once again, these deficits were met by international borrowing, but in an environment of high and rising interest rates this soon provoked one of the sharpest financial crises of the century, which is discussed later in this chapter. In the meantime, the new regime of flexible exchange rates posed challenges for international economic relations.

Operation of floating exchange rates

When the Bretton Woods era of pegged exchange rates finally had to be abandoned in the spring of 1973, there was still not a complete consensus that floating exchange rates were the best option. As noted above, the final formal acceptance of the status quo was only reached by the IMF in 1976. For most countries, pegged regimes remained desirable to prevent desta-bilising fluctuations in real producer and consumer incomes. Most countries did not have a foreign exchange market that was deep or broad enough to operate freely floating regimes and many countries wanted to retain capital controls that ruled out floating. The problem for many states was how to sustain stable exchange rates in an increasingly volatile environment. Pegging to the US dollar was difficult to sustain in the inflationary environ-ment early in the 1970s when dollar depreciation added to inflationary pressure, and then again from 1974, when following the US dollar apprecia-tion choked export competitiveness. The problems of managing a bilateral peg encouraged many countries such as Australia, New Zealand and Malaysia to adopt pegs to a trade-weighted basket of currencies in the 1970s. This type of regime was designed to stabilise the effective exchange rate, which more closely matched the actual pattern of a country's international transactions.

Many core industrial countries tended to operate flexible exchange rate regimes with a range of freedom extending from the United States, which practiced a policy of non-intervention or benign neglect, to the UK, which tried (often unsuccessfully) to target the sterling–dollar exchange rate within moving bands while nominally floating. The difference between *de jure* and *de facto* regimes (or between what countries say they do and what they actually do) became more distinct and has since complicated analyses of the effectiveness of different regimes. As noted above, floating or even flexible exchange rates did not suit the majority of states. Within Europe, the momentum toward greater exchange rate stability had gathered force at the end of the 1960s when it seemed the world was about to embark on an era of greater flexibility. For EEC countries, the costs of exchange rate instability were too high to join this trend, and they sought ways to co-ordinate their exchange rate policy.

We have seen in Chapter 3 that at the Hague Summit in 1969 it was decided that the EEC should gradually transform itself into an Economic and Monetary Union (EMU). The timescale was set by the Werner Committee, which met in 1970 and set a goal of ten years for the transition to EMU. This implied a currency union among members, which would eliminate internal exchange rate movements by instituting a single currency or irretrievably fixed exchange rates, requiring the co-ordination of economic policies and so moving on to the fourth level of economic integration. This initiative was ill-fated as the Werner Committee's timetable was agreed in 1971 just in time for the collapse of the Bretton Woods system and then the oil crisis of 1973. The international economic environment was too turbulent to allow real progress on policy co-ordination or joint-policy making even among the

European Community (EC), and the plans were quietly abandoned in 1973, although monetary union remained an ultimate goal.

Meanwhile, the EC was enlarged with the addition of the UK, Ireland and Denmark in 1973, followed by Greece in 1981 and Spain and Portugal in 1986. The greater diversity of the expanded membership of the EC further complicated the potential for the policy co-ordination necessary for EMU. The UK had close economic links outside Europe, while the new entrants from southern Europe were at a different stage of economic development from the original six members, with large agricultural sectors and lower incomes per capita. In March 1979 an alternative and more modest European Monetary System (EMS) was launched, although EMU remained the long-term goal. The EMS was meant to breathe new life into the integration process, which had stalled during the decade of stagflation. It established a unit of account called the European Currency Unit (ECU) for EC transactions, which was valued as a weighted basket of participating currencies. Members would peg their exchange rates to the ECU (with margins of ±2.25 per cent for fluctuations) and so adhere to an Exchange Rate Mechanism (ERM) to draw European exchange rates into a co-ordinated framework. In addition, members contributed 20 per cent of their gold and foreign exchange reserves to a common reserves fund. The EMS was more modest than the EMU, seeking a zone of monetary stability rather than immutable exchange rates or a common currency, but it was seen by some as a stepping stone toward full economic integration. The value of the ECU was heavily weighted toward the Deutschmark, which comprised almost one third of the total value. The French franc was the second largest determinant of the ECU's value, with almost 20 per cent of the weight. Although Britain did not take part in the EMS, the pound did form part of the valuation of the ECU, with 13 per cent of the weight. The bias toward the Deutschemark meant that, in practice, members of the ERM were required to follow the interest rate and inflation policies of the West German government and Bundesbank in order to retain their exchange rate stability. While the West German economy was among the most stable and prosperous in Europe, this was advantageous to participating countries. As we shall see in Chapter 5, however, once the German economy as the anchor to the system began to falter, the EMS became unstable. While Europe tried to use closer economic integration to sustain its economic performance, the difficulties of developing economies were starkly revealed by the economic crises of the 1970s.

Problems of unequal development

We have seen that the gap between rich and poor countries widened during the rapid growth era of the 1960s. This process was exacerbated by the economic turmoil of the 1970s despite a range of efforts to redress what was emerging clearly as a structural problem. The effort to reach out to sustain links between the EC and former colonial territories in Africa – begun with the Yaounde Convention in 1963 – was extended in 1975 by the first Lome Convention between the EC and forty-six African, Caribbean and Pacific states. This extended trade preferences to a range of commonwealth countries and former European colonies to allow them preferential access to EC markets for their products. Nevertheless, the share of Africa in global trade did not materially improve during the 1970s, remaining at about 4 per cent despite oil exploitation in Nigeria. The share of non-OPEC developing economies as a whole in world trade also remained fairly constant during the 1970s at about 13 per cent of global trade, having fallen from 27 per cent in 1955 to 15 per cent in 1965 according to UNCTAD.

The tendency of economies that rely on natural resource exploitation to grow relatively slowly and also for these states to be prone to internal conflict has been identified as a 'resource curse'. Reliance on exporting a single commodity means that foreign income becomes vulnerable to fluctuations in world prices, which can lead to volatile government, as well as private, revenues. The operation of foreign companies and the liquid nature of contracts may also increase the vulnerability of the state and business to corruption. Flows of wealth from resource exploitation may also reduce incentives to promote reform of fundamental institutions such as welfare or education that would help to diversify the economy. Economies such as Nigeria, Sierra Leone, Angola and Venezuela are sometimes grouped into this category. On the other hand, it is clear that many resource-dependent economies with better institutions have successfully sustained high per capita incomes and stable political systems, while achieving greater diversification of production – examples including Botswana, Norway, Canada and Australia. This paradox has been debated since the 1950s and remains controversial.[1]

The impact of the oil crisis on the gap between rich and poor nations was two-fold. First, the oil crisis hit less developed countries most severely, both directly in terms of the cost of imports and also indirectly as demand for their primary products was reduced due to the global recession. Second, the success of OPEC showed the vulnerability of the developed world to raw material producers if they were able to organise cartels, and this danger renewed interest among rich countries in promoting global development. The Sixth Special Session of the United Nations General Assembly in 1974 (the first to deal exclusively with economic issues) adopted two resolutions that became the platform for a New International Economic Order (NIEO), which ambitiously aimed:

... to work urgently for the establishment of a NIEO based on equity, sovereign equality, common interest and cooperation among all states ... correct inequalities and redress existing injustices, make it possible to eliminate the widening gap between the developed and the developing countries and ensure steadily accelerating economic and social development and peace and justice for present and future generations.

This was followed by the United Nations Charter of Economic Rights and Duties in December 1974 and a series of other announcements, agreements and conferences throughout the 1970s, which ultimately failed in their goal of reducing the gap between rich and poor states.

The ideology behind these initiatives was to some extent based on a doctrine first espoused by Raoul Prebisch in the late 1940s: that there is an inevitable adverse trend in the terms of trade of primary commodities resulting in a bias in favour of industrial producers. This is because of the low income elasticity of demand for raw materials; as income rises the share spent on food and raw materials falls but the demand for services and manufactures increases. In the post-1945 decades, this trend was enhanced by raw-material-saving technology, such as artificial rubber and textiles. Prebisch suggested that as world production and incomes increased, primary products would play a diminishing role and thus less-industrialised countries would not share equally in global economic growth. This diagnosis prompted a call for efforts to ensure equal access to global markets for poor countries and pro-active policies to increase industrialisation in these countries, perhaps through aid or loans, protecting infant industrial sectors with trade barriers and more central planning and co-ordination by governments. At the same time, however, the stagflation challenge was pushing governments in core industrial countries such as the US and the UK toward more free market, small government ideologies, such as neo-classical economics and monetarism. This contrast between economic ideologies in the developed and developing world provoked further conflict in global policy-making.

A further element contributing to unequal growth was agricultural protectionism in many industrialised countries, which constrained the market for food produced by many poorer countries. Agricultural tariffs were high in all industrialised countries, but the most comprehensive example in the 1970s was the CAP of the EEC. Table 4.2 shows the impact of the common external tariff on agricultural prices in Europe.

The gap between European and world prices fell for many products during the 1970s, but it remained extraordinarily high for particular products such as butter and beef. Other examples of agricultural protection among industrial countries included Japanese beef and rice and American cotton and sugar. Many producers of food and materials in industrial countries

Table 4.2 EC prices as a per cent of world market prices

	1968–72	1973–7	1978–80
Hard wheat	222	167	171
Rice	171	117	129
Sugar	247	129	165
Beef	140	171	198
Barley	174	135	173
Butter	404	349	367
Pork	140	123	147

Note: World prices are depressed by EC dumping.

Source: W. Molle, *The Economics of European Integration*, Dartmouth Publishing Co., 1990.

were protected through various forms of domestic subsidies for producers, tariffs, quotas and other non-tariff barriers, as well as through export subsidies that gave producers an unfair competitive edge on the international market. It was not until the Uruguay Round of GATT from 1995 that agriculture became the focus of reducing barriers to trade.

An alternative explanation for the persistent gap in global income was political instability and conflict in many poor countries that bred corruption and inefficiency, as well as inhibiting the improvement of growth-inducing institutions such as education, health care and gender equality, with disastrous consequences for local populations. In the end, the much-vaunted NIEO was a failure partly because of a lack of resources and commitment among rich countries preoccupied with their own economic prospects, and partly because of continued military conflict and institutional barriers to development in less developed states. Developing economies' per capita GDP increased from 7 per cent of developed countries to 8 per cent from 1970–9, but this included oil exporters. Non-oil developing countries' GDP per capita fell from 7 per cent of developed countries to 6 per cent according to UNCTAD figures.

Despite the generally poor relative performance of developing economies, there were pockets of optimism. Several economies in East Asia achieved a rapid industrialisation in the 1960s and 1970s based on export-led growth by concentrating first on labour-intensive production of cheap manufactures and then on higher value-added exports. The key leaders were Taiwan (Republic of China), South Korea, Hong Kong and Singapore, which contributed to a sharp rise in the share of East Asia in world trade over this period. In the 1980s the World Bank labelled the success of these 'four Asian tigers' an 'economic miracle', but the causes of their growth were more prosaic (and ultimately more fragile) than this description suggests.

Close relations between the state and industry in the cases of Taiwan, South Korea and Singapore channelled capital toward industrial exporters and helped them achieve economies of scale quickly. Singapore, and to a lesser extent Hong Kong, exploited their relatively cheap labour to attract multinational companies and to produce a range of inexpensive manufactures including textiles, toys and plastic goods during the 1960s. During the boom years of that decade, these four export-orientated economies established themselves as keen competitors in global markets, taking 3.8 per cent of world exports in 1980 compared with 1.5 per cent in 1965.

The 1970s were more challenging for these industrialising states as the global recession required domestic restructuring, but again the close relations between government and industrialists eased the transition, particularly for South Korea, Taiwan and Singapore. South Korea successfully made the transition to heavy industry, including steel and shipbuilding, in this decade, while Singapore and Hong Kong exploited their location, regulatory and cultural advantages to promote their financial services sectors, taking advantage of the rapid expansion and innovation in international finance. The strategy of attracting multinational companies (in the case of Taiwan and Singapore) or using sovereign international borrowing for development rather than for consumption (in the case of South Korea) helped to insulate these states somewhat from the impact of the developing-country debt crisis that loomed by the end of the 1970s.

This success contrasted sharply with the experience in many Latin American countries where regimes eschewed international trade in favour of protectionist industrialisation strategies, which ultimately failed to provide sustained growth. Weak institutions such as property rights or the rule of law promoted corruption and flight of capital as rich residents invested their capital outside their home country. This left many states reliant on foreign borrowing and vulnerable to shifts in global investor sentiment.

Rise of sovereign debt and the Third World Debt Crisis

The problems of unequal growth set the stage for the Third World Debt Crisis of 1982. The crisis was sparked by the Mexican government's announcement in New York on 20 August 1982 that it proposed to default on its sovereign debt and demanded that creditors reschedule. In 1981 alone, Mexico's debt had increased from US$55 billion to $80 billion. Its announcement was quickly repeated by other countries including Argentina, Brazil and Chile and sparked a global financial shock as the world's banks scrambled to reassess their balance sheets. The crisis had arisen due both to the demand for loans and the supply of lending over the previous decade.

The demand for loans among developing countries arose from the need to fund increasing current account deficits, especially after the oil price shock of 1973–4. The oil crisis prompted deficits even in middle-income oil producing states such as Mexico and Nigeria as inflation and consumption surged. The Mexican government was particularly optimistic and increased borrowing sharply after 1979 to engage in oil exploration. Overall, outstanding debt in developing countries exploded from US$68 billion in 1970 to $546 billion by 1982. To be sustainable, overseas borrowing should be either short term to smooth over consumption in the expectation of a reversal of the deficit, or self-financing, usually through investing the funds in enterprises that will in time generate foreign exchange revenue to service and ultimately repay the debt. Borrowing with an obligation to repay on demand and using the funds for investments that would only produce an income in the longer term is known as maturity mismatch, which leaves countries vulnerable if creditors suddenly recall their loans. Another vulnerability is currency mismatch, where governments have an obligation to repay dollars but their income is mainly denominated in the domestic currency. If the domestic currency is devalued, it becomes even more expensive to repay the loan. South Korea was the world's fourth-largest sovereign debtor in 1982 due to the government's strategy of borrowing funds for industrial enterprises rather than relying on foreign multinational companies for capital. Foreign debt rose from 7 per cent of GNP in 1965 to 25 per cent by 1970 and then to over 50 per cent by 1983.[2] At the same time, the cost of servicing that debt (including interest and capital payments) rose from 2 per cent of export earnings in 1965 to 14 per cent by 1983. The robustness of the South Korean economy and the appetite for its exports, however, allowed South Korea to trade its way out of debt since the borrowing had been invested in export-orientated production. Such was not the case for many states in Latin America. The Mexican government borrowed heavily from 1979 on the expectation of future oil revenues, but when the oil price began to fall in late 1981 the debt service burden began to race ahead of the ability to repay. The situation was exacerbated by capital flight so that by the end 1981, private overseas assets totalled US$10 billion (mainly in bank accounts overseas owned by Mexicans). In February 1982 the Mexican peso was allowed to depreciate and lost 40 per cent of its value against the US dollar within a week, further increasing the burden of debt, which was denominated in US dollars.

On the other side, there were certainly errors in the supply of loans. Several factors came together to increase lending in the 1970s. First, the huge surpluses of OPEC states tended to be accumulated in bank accounts and other reserves rather than spent on imports. With political friction between the Middle East and the United States, many OPEC states chose to deposit their US dollar in banks in Europe, thus swelling the amount of so-called 'Eurodollars', as US dollar deposits outside the United States became known. Meanwhile, the global recession reduced demand for loans in rich countries and left large banks with substantial excess liquidity. In 1974 the American government removed controls on exports of capital and this allowed the on-lending of the banks' surplus deposits to willing borrowers overseas, particularly in Latin America. Commercial bank lending for development was encouraged by governments who sought to reduce their aid budgets during the recession. By 1982 the nine largest US banks had loans outstanding to Latin American borrowers that were equivalent to 176 per cent of their combined capital and reserves. Clearly these banks were exposed to a substantial risk if borrowers defaulted on these loans.

Given the global recession and potential instability, why did banks lend so liberally to developing economies when in hindsight the prospects for repayment seem poor? There were a range of market factors that shifted the assessment of risk in international lending in the 1970s. First, there was increased loan syndication that allowed groups of banks to share the risk burden of a loan. As each individual bank appeared less exposed to default, this may have encouraged larger and more risky lending overall. Second, the loans were to governments rather than businesses and it seems that the default risk of states was underestimated. There were sophisticated analyses of the credit-worthiness of businesses and the ability to retrieve assets after receivership, but the prospects that an entire country would default appeared to be less likely. Sovereign risk is difficult to assess because the economies do not actually go bankrupt – a government chooses when to default. In this event there are no assets to seize, but lenders may have expectations that international organizations such as the IMF or World Bank will assist states in default by lending or granting them funds to repay their debts. The expectation that the losses might be shared *ex post* with another body introduced what is known as 'moral hazard' and encouraged more risky lending. Third, there had been a dramatic expansion in international financial activity in the 1960s and 1970s that drew new lenders into the market over the decade. A loan in 1970 might have been rational for the individual bank at the time, but it was made more risky by subsequent lending from other banks that increased the prospect of an overall default. In this way, the rapid accumulation of lending reduced the security of existing loans.

This description of the failure of lenders to assess the risk of their lending adequately opens the question of the effectiveness of prudential supervision of international banking in the run up to the 1982 crisis. Should the authorities be partly blamed for allowing the accumulation of large debts that posed systemic risk for the global banking system as a whole? In 1974, a run on several international banks after losses on foreign exchange positions prompted central bankers to consider whether and how to regulate and supervise the ballooning market in international finance. The failure of the Herstatt Bank in West Germany, the Anglo-Israeli Bank in London and the Franklin National Bank in the United States exposed confusion over which jurisdiction was responsible for supervising and bailing out the increasingly global international banking market. In 1975 the Basel Committee on Banking Supervision was established to consider into which jurisdiction branches and subsidiaries should fall for supervision: was it the responsibility of the host centre or the centre where the parent company was registered? A further question was how to increase the flow of information on lending and borrowing to enhance transparency, but little progress was achieved in collecting and publishing sovereign debt exposure of borrowers until the late 1970s. The distribution of the loan portfolios of individual banks was considered private commercial information that needed to be protected and there was resistance by banks and also by regulators to publish this data. From the late 1970s, however, consolidated sovereign lending data were published to help inform the assessment of the risk of new lending. In the end, this was too little too late to prevent the crisis of 1982.

There were clearly faults on the part of borrowers as well as lenders that allowed the crisis to develop, but there were also precipitating environmental factors. An increasing amount of lending was at floating interest rates through the 1970s, which meant that the interest rate risk was passed on to the borrower. This made lending seem less risky to banks, but it eventually increased the risk that the borrower would be unable to pay – particularly once Paul Volcker as Chairman of the Federal Reserve raised interest rates dramatically to contain US inflation. In August 1979 US interest rates were 9.5 per cent, but they increased sharply in response to the second oil crisis to 16 per cent by May 1981. The cost of servicing existing debt was further increased by the appreciation of the US dollar by 25 per cent from 1980–2. In 1975 the debt service on long-term borrowing by developing countries equalled about 9 per cent of these countries' export revenue, but by 1982 this had reached 15.5 per cent (according to UNCTAD figures).

Table 4.3 shows changes in the nature of borrowing during the 1970s up to the outbreak of the crisis. The share of total long-term loans to governments rather than private borrowers rose from 75 per cent to 83 per cent, so the sovereign debt share increased over time. Borrowing from official sources such as foreign governments fell from over half of all lending to 37 per cent, while borrowing from private lenders increased sharply from one fifth to almost one half of the total. Of this, commercial banks were the most important lenders with a share of only 6 per cent of long-term lending to developing countries in 1970, but 31 per cent by 1982

Table 4.3 Developing country indebtedness 1970–82: Share of total long-term debt (%)

	1970	1975	1979	1982
Total public and publicly guaranteed debt	74.9	78.9	84.5	83.1
Total official creditors	53.9	46.3	38.3	37.3
Of which bilateral creditors	41.6	34.2	26.3	24.5
Of which multilateral creditors	12.3	12.0	12.0	12.8
Total private creditors	20.9	32.6	46.2	45.8
Bonds	3.1	1.9	3.8	4.0
Commercial banks	6.3	19.5	30.1	30.9
Other private credits	11.5	11.2	12.3	11.0
Total private nonguaranteed debt	25.1	21.1	15.5	16.9

Source: UNCTAD, *Handbook of Statistics*

(39 per cent for South American borrowers). The massive redistribution of global capital certainly eased the adjustment to the oil price increases and global recession for developing countries in the medium term, but it proved ultimately unsustainable, and in the 1980s their economies were forced to undergo painful restructuring.

Mexico's default in August 1982 spread shock and fear through the global financial system as lending to all developing countries immediately appeared at risk. The problem seemed analogous to the 1930s Great Depression when defaults on US bank mortgages and falling land prices stripped the value of banks' assets and sparked a damaging banking crisis. A stylised example shows that a solvency crisis arises once the value of the loan portfolio of a bank is reduced. Banks take in deposits from the public, which then appear as liabilities on their balance sheet; banks have a liability to repay depositors on demand. The business of banking is to take these funds and lend them out at a profitable interest; these loans then appear as assets on the bank's balance sheet. If the value of these loans suddenly becomes worthless because the creditor defaults, the bank has no assets to repay depositors. In the 1930s this led to a run on the banking system as depositors raced to withdraw their cash deposits, prompting the closure of many banks across the United States. To prevent a repeat of this chaos, the US government introduced federal deposit insurance to reassure depositors. In the 1980s, therefore, a run on the banks was not the first challenge to the banking system, but the huge write-down of the value of the banks' assets threatened to freeze up domestic and international bank lending. Also, since the deposit insurance shifted the burden of repaying depositors to the government, both the banks and the US government had an incentive to prop up the nominal value of developing-country debt in banks' balance sheets and thus avoid an ultimate default that would wipe out the value of these loans. The other main player was the IMF, who sought to sustain the development and financial stability of its member countries.

There was a range of solutions to the crisis. The first approach was to bring creditor and debtor together to scale down and reschedule payments on the debt to avoid outright default and thereby sustain banks' balance sheets. These negotiations happened often on a trilateral level between the debtor, the bank and the IMF as broker. In addition there was the Paris Club of official government lenders that negotiated with many of the poorest countries in the world to re-schedule their debt. In 1983 sixteen arrangements were concluded with African and Latin American states re-scheduling US\$9.545 billion of debt, over a third of which was for Brazil. The involvement of the IMF was controversial since it offered to extend further credit to countries only once they had come to a settlement with their bank creditors that included new bridging loans, and so long as they agreed to restructuring programmes to get their economies onto a more sustainable basis. Commercial banks were often more willing to conclude generous agreements to reschedule debt once they knew that their customer would soon be eligible for further IMF support. This network of relationships prompted claims that the IMF was causing moral hazard and sustaining a myth of the amount of debt that could realistically be repaid.[3] From another perspective, the IMF was heavily criticised for imposing strict adjustment programmes, including fiscal and monetary tightening, wage controls and currency devaluation, on economies that were already poor and struggling with weak institutional foundations to implement reform. In the end, the programmes proved very problematic for many countries due to political and technical obstacles.

These were the short-term fixes that postponed debt repayments in the hope that longer-term structural reform would allow a final resolution to the credit-worthiness of borrowers, but this left the global system in a precarious position in the medium term. From 1984 the IMF brokered Multi-Year Rescheduling Agreements (MYRAs) to replace annual negotiations, which reduced some uncertainty and allowed the banks more time to repair their balance sheets by accumulating other assets. In the meantime, however, lending to developing countries was beginning to fall, which threatened their longer-term development. In October 1985 the US initiated the Baker Plan (named for the US Treasury Secretary James Baker) to encourage banks to resume lending to fifteen heavily indebted countries. The plan called for structural reform of the economies of these debtors, including financial liberalisation and market-promoting reforms to increase private sector savings and investment as well as continued surveillance by the IMF. The target was for banks to resume lending up to US$20 billion. At the same time, the World Bank and other multilateral institutions were urged to increase their loans and aid by US$27 billion to match this commitment. The goal was to allow countries to grow out of their debt. By 1988 the World Bank had met its targets of disbursements, but net new lending by commercial banks was less easy to achieve, although gross flows did come close meeting the Baker Plan targets on some measures.[4] The outcome for growth was less optimistic, with increases of only 2.5 per cent for the Baker fifteen from 1986–8, although this reversed a decline from 1981–3. The path was not an easy one; in February 1987, Brazil imposed a moratorium on interest payments on its commercial debt, and as noted above, the implementation of restructuring programmes proved problematic for many states. Gradually, consensus built up that debt relief was needed to bring a final resolution to the problems of heavily indebted developing countries.

Partial debt relief agreements were successfully negotiated for Bolivia and Mexico in 1987–8, and these were used as a model for the Brady Plan introduced in 1989 (named for the new US Treasury Secretary Nicholas Brady). Brady was quoted by *Time* magazine on 20 March 1989 that:

> Our objective is to rekindle the hope of the people and leaders of debtor nations that their sacrifices will lead to greater prosperity in the present and the prospect of a future unclouded by the burden of debt.

The plan provided for countries to 'buy back' their debt using special funds from the IMF in addition to the usual stand-by arrangements associated with restructuring programmes. Commercial bank creditors were offered a 'menu' of alternative ways to reduce the burden, including accepting payment on the (discounted) market value of sovereign debt rather than the original value of the asset, and swapping existing loans for equity in companies or other negotiable dollar denominated bonds, known as Brady Bonds. A secondary market for Brady Bonds allowed banks to move these assets off their balance sheets. These arrangements were attractive to the banks, who sought to eliminate the bad debts on their balance sheets and for the debtors, who sought to remove the outstanding claims on future foreign exchange earnings. Mexico concluded the first Brady Plan agreement in 1989 with a valuation of existing debt of US$49 billion representing on average about 55 per cent of face value, with a range of buy-back deals and exchange of debt for Brady Bonds. Mexico's last Brady Bonds were retired in 2003. Other deals were more generous; Costa Rica, for example, paid only 16 cents on the dollar for 60 per cent of its nominal total debt of US$1.8 billion in 1990 while the rest was swapped for equity and Brady Bonds. About seventeen countries issued Brady Bonds under the scheme, and on average the deals wrote off about 30–35 per cent of the value of outstanding debt, thus reducing the burden of these countries significantly and setting the foundation for renewed growth in many emerging markets in the 1990s.

While borrowers in default were encouraged to restructure their debt and reform their economic systems, the apparent imprudence on the part of bank lenders also attracted attention. At the Bank for International Settlements (BIS), the efforts of the Basel Committee to standardise the rules of supervision and enhance risk management were hampered by the fact that control of national banking and financial systems was a jealously guarded element of each state's national sovereignty. As the chairman of the Basel Committee, George Blunden of the Bank of England, stated in 1977:

> The banking system of a country is central to the management and efficiency of its economy; its supervision will inevitably be a jealously guarded national prerogative. Its subordination to an international authority is a highly unlikely development, which would require a degree of political commitment which neither exists nor is conceivable in the foreseeable future.[5]

The debt crisis five years later showed the vulnerability of national banking systems to systemic international crises and led to greater focus on developing common standards to reduce exposure to sovereign debt risk in the future. In 1987 the Basel Committee published a consultative paper on rules for the amount of capital reserves that should be held by banks against sovereign lending to try to reduce the risk of bank failure in case of default. These rules were adopted by many banking regulators in 1992, but as we will see in Chapter 5, this was just in time for the next round of crises in emerging markets in the 1990s. The weakness of international financial regulation that underlay the 2007–8 global financial crises was already well established by the 1980s.

Conclusions and summary

The decade of turmoil in the 1970s, with the advent of flexible exchange rates and inflationary commodity price shocks, had long-lasting effects on international economic relations as well as on the relative fortunes of developing and developed nations. The accumulation of debt during this decade took twenty years to unwind and plagued the development aspirations of many countries. The shock of unemployment and inflation during this period certainly made the era from 1955–70 appear in retrospect one of stability and prosperity, which it seemed might not be repeated within the next generation. It was in the 1980s that the post-war years became known as a 'golden age of capitalism' or the 'long boom'. This challenge prompted a seminal shift in economic ideology that affected economic policy-making through the next twenty years, launching the second era of globalisation by the 1990s.

5 The start of the second globalisation 1985–95

After the economic crises of the 1970s, in the 1980s the dominant economic ideology shifted toward the promotion of more open markets for both finance and merchandise trade. Along with innovation in financial services and communications technology, this change in policy emphasis prompted the beginning of a new era of globalisation arising from the integration of trade and financial flows. The economic benefits of more open markets for growth seemed intuitively compelling, reinforced by the success of several newly industrialising East Asian countries, which appeared to offer a model of export-led growth for other developing countries to emulate. The globalisation process soon became controversial, however, once the persistence of uneven economic growth and the failure of market integration to generate income convergence became apparent.

Ideology of globalisation

A defining characteristic of the 1980s and 1990s was the renewed globalisation of the international economy. This phenomenon was much discussed at the time, prompting claims that it led to the exploitation of poor countries, reduced the integrity of cultural distinctions and undermined national identities.[1] On the other hand, champions of globalisation praised the economic, cultural and social benefits of easier global communications and financial flows. In the process, the concept of globalisation itself became somewhat blurred. A reasonable interpretation for our purposes is that 'globalisation' identified the progressive integration of markets among a wide range of global participants. This took place on a range of platforms including economically, through trade and migration, and financially, through open capital markets. Cultural globalisation included the expansion of multinational companies spreading common working practices, common consumption patterns (such as MacDonalds or Tesco) and, of course, access to common media, TV, movies and music through the internet and other avenues of global distribution. Did this prompt the end of the 'local' or 'regional' identity as the global population shared more in common, or was it a launch-pad for distinctive local and regional culture to influence a global audience? These questions are still contested, but this chapter will deal primarily with how globalisation was manifested in international economic relations rather than the cultural phenomena, although of course they are closely linked.

One of the first important observations is that the 1980s saw the *return* of globalisation rather than its launch. International economic relations had followed a U-shaped pattern with high levels of intense international interaction in the mid and late nineteenth century followed by a retreat in international trade, investment and migration during the inter-war Great Depression and post-war recovery. While merchandise trade was liberalised during the 1950s and 1960s particularly for manufactures (although less so for agricultural products), capital flows remained tightly controlled. A key feature of the Bretton Woods ideology was that freer trade was vital to the prosperity of the global economy, but that free international capital flows threatened each state's ability to sustain the pegged exchange rate system at the same time as pursuing expansionary economic policies aimed at full employment. Financial flows were associated with damaging speculation that undermined national goals of full employment and price stability.

Once the constraint of the pegged exchange rate regime was relaxed from the early 1970s, some countries moved to floating or flexible exchange rates and reduced or removed capital controls. This was most marked for the United States, which abandoned most capital controls in 1974. The UK already had very open international financial markets in their offshore Eurodollar market and by 1979 had abandoned exchange controls on sterling transactions also. Other countries opted to continue with a range of pegged exchange rate regimes either to trade-weighted baskets or, in the case of European states, more complete monetary integration. With this mixture of exchange rate regimes, we need to be careful in characterising the movement from a pegged rate system in the 1960s through to a more flexible rate system in the 1980s. Figure 5.1 shows the actual rather than official exchange rate regimes operated by the world's economies, calculated by Reinhart and Rogoff, which emphasises the mixture of various degrees of pegged or managed exchange rates and the very small number of states that allowed their exchange rate to float even in the 1980s. This contrasts with how countries reported their regimes to the IMF, which suggested that almost a quarter of countries were operating floating exchange rates by the early 1980s compared with only 3 per cent when measuring actual exchange rate performance. It was clearly difficult for governments to abandon their exchange rate as a tool of policy, and most officially floating regimes were actually managed pegs or target bands.

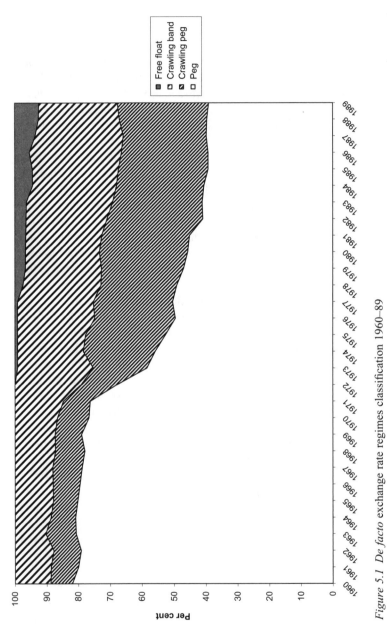

Figure 5.1 De facto exchange rate regimes classification 1960–89

Source: C.M. Reinhart and K.S. Rogoff, 'The modern history of exchange rate arrangements: a reinterpretation,' *Quarterly Journal of Economics*, 119, 1 (February), pp. 1–48 (excludes currencies in free fall).

A new era of globalisation was finally possible from the mid-1980s, once most countries had achieved more reliable economic recovery from the turmoil of the 1970s and the inflationary spiral of that decade had been broken. There was a range of factors contributing to the growing intensity of international economic relations. A first element was the dominance in many countries of a neo-liberal political leadership that promoted market-based reforms – most starkly marked by the radical conservative administrations of Prime Minister Margaret Thatcher in the UK and President Ronald Reagan in the United States. This ideological shift arose from the challenges of stagflation in the 1970s, which discredited the Keynesian demand management policies that had prevailed as the dominant economic paradigm since the 1950s. The success of Federal Reserve Chairman Paul Volcker's use of high interest rates to combat inflation in the United States after 1979 added further credibility to the new monetarist economics. At the same time, European states sought to sustain their economic recovery by continuing the process of market integration, signing the Single European Act in 1986 to form a common market in goods, people, services and capital by 1992. The ideological shift spread to developing economies through multilateral institutions such as the IMF and the World Bank, which tended in the 1980s to promote market liberalisation (including devaluation, financial liberalisation and freer trade) as part of their economic support programmes. This approach proved controversial and was identified as a 'Washington Consensus'[2] that failed to recognise the institutional obstacles for many developing countries in adopting freer markets when property rights were weak and there were significant gaps between rich and poor. These obstacles posed transitional costs, both economic and political, in implementing the policies recommended by the World Bank and the IMF.

In addition to changes in economic policy, the pace of innovation in communications technology such as satellite communications, fax, information technology, and of course by the 1990s the World Wide Web helped to reduce international transaction costs. For example, the first transatlantic fibre-optic cable was completed in 1988, carrying four times as many channels as its predecessor. There was also innovation in production and managerial processes that enhanced the effectiveness of transnational corporations and encouraged them to spread the geographical reach of their activities. Containerisation of cargo and the use of information and communications technology (ICT) in global supply chain management hugely increased the efficiency of international freight and streamlined the transition from ship to rail or road. The UN estimated that the cost of insurance and freight amounted to 4.7 per cent of manufactures trade in 1980 but only 3.6 per cent by 1990.[3] Nevertheless, empirical evidence about the relative importance of tariff reduction, transport cost reduction and growth of incomes as alternative explanations of the expansion of world trade have shown that income growth and market liberalisation were probably the most important factors.[4] While nineteenth-century globalisation was mainly driven by reduced transport costs for people and goods over long distances, the second globalisation was driven by the liberalisation of markets as well as innovations in communications and transport.

Measuring globalisation

Globalisation can be measured across a range of international economic relations: international trade, international investment and international migration. During the first era of globalisation in the late nineteenth century the redistribution of people from Europe to North and South America as well as intra-Asian migration were important features generating global integration, particularly as unskilled labour moved out of industrialised economies to other regions. The UN calculated that in 2000, one in thirty-five of the world's population was living outside the country in which they had been born. The ratio for 1910, near the end of the first era of globalisation, was only one in forty-eight people.[5] While international migration in the second era of globalisation appears to have been more intense, it also had very distinctive characteristics that affected its impact. Net migration into developed countries increased from about one per thousand inhabitants in the 1960s to 2.5 per thousand in the 1990s. Net migration from developing countries, however, remained at the low level of less than 0.5 per thousand inhabitants, emphasising that labour mobility and migration were primarily a feature of richer societies rather than a source of opportunity for poorer populations, as had been the case in the nineteenth century.

Table 5.1 shows that the share of migrants in national populations did not change much from 1960 to 2000 for the world as a whole and that there was a concentration of migration to wealthy countries such as the United States, Canada and Australia.

Migration was particularly important for Australia, where 22 per cent of residents were foreign-born in 1989–90, rising to almost 24 per cent by 1999. Most of these immigrants had been born in the UK or Ireland, and migrants made up a quarter of the Australian work force.[6] By the end of the 1990s the median age of British immigrants to Australia was fifty, suggesting that most were arriving to retire or finish their careers. Those arriving from East and Southeast Asia, however, tended to be much younger (in their late twenties and early thirties), suggesting they were coming to make their livelihoods in Australia. The most common professions were managers, IT specialists and accountants, in line with controls that favoured

Table 5.1 International migrants as a share of the population, 1960 and 2000 (%)

	1960	2000
World	2.5	2.9
Developed countries (incl. USSR)	3.4	8.7
Developed countries (excl. USSR)	4.0	8.3
Developing countres	2.1	1.3
Africa	3.2	2.0
Asia	1.8	1.2
Latin America and Caribbean	2.8	1.1
Northern America	6.1	12.9
Oceania	13.4	18.8
Europe	3.3	6.4
Former USSR	1.4	10.2

Source: UN, *World Economic and Social Survey*, 2004

entry of skilled migrants. As one of the richest countries in the Asia-Pacific region (after Japan) the share of immigrants to Australia born in Asia rose from about 5 per cent in the 1960s to 51 per cent by the early 1990s.

As in the late nineteenth century, the United States was the largest single target for international migrants, accounting for 13 per cent of the migrant stock in 1960 and 20 per cent by 2000. The share of foreign-born residents in the total population increased from 9 per cent in 1990 to 13 per cent by 2005. This reflected the large size of the US economy, the relatively high incomes there and rapid growth in the 1990s, which opened up new opportunities. In addition to the recorded migrants, an estimated 7 million unauthorised migrants, mainly from Mexico, are estimated to have settled to work in mainly unskilled employment in the United States.[7]

Restrictions on international migration imposed by developed countries in the twentieth century reduced the potential for population flows to shrink global income inequalities. By the 1990s it was mainly skilled workers who had the opportunity to move rather than unskilled workers from poorer countries who might hope to raise their prospects through migration. Skilled workers emigrating would tend to raise the incomes of those skilled workers who remained, while unskilled workers with more limited mobility tended to see their wages depressed. Additionally, a brain-drain of educated, skilled labour, such as doctors and nurses, could undermine the development prospects of poorer countries. On the other hand, remittances home have increased with the stock of migrants, and by the mid-1990s these remittances exceeded inflows of official development assistance, becoming an important source of income and foreign exchange for many developing countries. In 2002, the EU was the largest source of remittances, followed by the United

States, while Mexico, India and the Philippines were the largest developing-country recipients.

The economic impact of international migration obviously differed according to region. Developed countries tend to have a slower natural rate of population increase, so immigrants were a more important source of population and labour force growth than was the case for developing countries. At the same time emigration from poorer countries tended not to decrease the rate of population growth substantially or make labour more scarce, which could have had a positive impact on incomes. By the mid-2000s the UN estimated that about 10 per cent of the population of richer countries were immigrants, while migrants only made up 1.5 per cent of the population of poor countries.[8]

While international migration was a major feature of these decades, the most common measures of globalisation are related to flows of goods and services. Figure 5.2 shows the rapid growth in the value of merchandise exports from the mid-1980s, and that this was due mainly to increases in trade among developed countries. The disappointing relative performance for developing states was due to falling prices for oil (after 1983) and other primary products such as cocoa and coffee.

The value of international trade relative to GDP was also distinctive between developed and developing states. Overall, trade in goods and services increased rapidly from 35 per cent to 40 per cent of global output from 1986 to 1990, but was considerably higher for developing countries where trade was 46 per cent of GDP in 1986 and reached 53 per cent by 1990. The importance of trade to the economy of the United States, the richest and most powerful economy in the world, was only about half of the world average, or about 20 per cent of GDP in the 1980s. By this measure, the United States was less connected to the process of trade globalisation than other countries. In Europe, the process of economic integration increased the share of trade in GDP to between 50 and 60 per cent in the 1980s.

Flows of trade and investment are clearly related, particularly through the expansion of transnational companies that spread the production of traded goods throughout the globe and thereby change the geographical distribution of trade. There is a range of connections between transnational companies and trade. The effect might be through the movement of inter-mediate goods and partly finished products between countries for processing in a form of supply-chain, which might include a range of companies located in different countries. Alternatively, an MNC might itself have ownership of resources, production, marketing and distribution in different countries so that goods might flow internationally but within the same company. By 1990 the OECD estimated that about one third of US exports

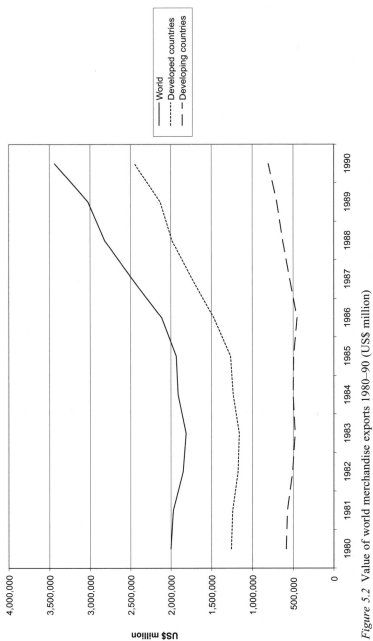

Figure 5.2 Value of world merchandise exports 1980–90 (US$ million)

Source: UNCTAD

and over 40 per cent of imports into the United States were accounted for by trade within firms. This compares to Japan where only about 17 per cent of exports and 15 per cent of imports were within firms.[9] Most intra-firm exports from the United States were by American companies that distributed their goods to other high-income markets through wholly owned subsidiaries or affiliates overseas. Also, unlike the first era of globalisation in the nineteenth century, most of the expansion of foreign investment in the 1980s flowed among developed nations rather than between developed and developing economies. Nevertheless, the overall surge in the value of foreign capital flows from 1980 did increase the value, if not the share, of investment in developing economies.

Figure 5.3 shows that the flow of foreign direct investment, which captures investment flows associated with transnational corporations, declined relative to international trade through the 1970s but then entered a sustained period of relative increase from 1983 to 1989. This increase in global foreign investment compared to international trade was a key distinguishing feature of the onset of the second globalisation.

Table 5.2 shows that between 1980 and 1990 the value of FDI flows quadrupled and then increased a further five-fold in the 1990s. In 1980, North America and Europe together accounted for almost 90 per cent of

Table 5.2 Foreign direct investment 1970–2005 (US$ million)

	1970	*1980*	*1990*	*2000*	*2005*
FDI inflows					
World	13,418	55,262	201,594	1,411,366	945,795
Developing economies	3,854	7,664	35,892	256,088	314,316
Economies in transition	24	75	9,040	41,169	
Developed economies	9,564	47,575	165,627	1,146,238	590,311
Europe	5,226	21,578	97,044	721,931	494,980
EU (25)	5,158	21,494	90,499	695,277	486,409
North America	3,083	22,725	56,004	380,802	129,947
FDI outflows					
World	12,151	53,829	229,598	1,239,190	837,194
Developing economies	51	3,153	11,913	133,341	115,860
Economies in transition	35	3,183	14,620		
Developed economies	12,100	50,676	217,649	1,102,666	706,713
Europe	5,095	24,126	129,857	866,241	691,217
EU (25)	5,063	23,872	121,238	811,669	608,799
North America	8,521	23,328	36,219	187,305	5,806

North America is the USA and Canada. 'Economies in transition' are those in Eastern Europe and Central Asia.

Source: UNCTAD, *Development and Globalization: Facts and Figures*, 2008

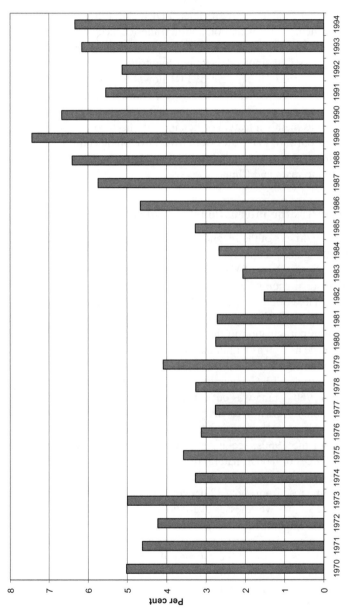

Figure 5.3 Global outward flows of FDI compared to exports 1970–95 (%)

Source: UNCTAD

FDI outflows and 80 per cent of inflows. The United States was the largest single source of foreign investment at the same time as being the largest target for foreign capital. Ten years later, FDI within Europe came to take a more prominent share of the total so that the EU accounted for 53 per cent of all outflows and 45 per cent of all inflows. The largest and fastest growing target for FDI among developing countries was East and Southeast Asia, which absorbed 10 per cent of FDI flows in 1990, particularly the high speed growth economies of South Korea, Taiwan, Singapore and Hong Kong. This evidence confirms the finding that globalisation of companies in the 1990s was mainly a feature of rich industrialised countries. By 2005, 14 per cent of outward FDI flows were from developing countries, but one quarter of this was flows of capital from Hong Kong special administrative region (SAR) to mainland China.

China re-enters the international economy

One of the key drivers of the second globalisation was the re-emergence of China into the global economy. During most of the post-1949 period, the Chinese Communist Party of Mao Zedong deliberately isolated the economy from international economic relations. Just as other Asian states such as Japan, Taiwan and South Korea were launching programmes of successful export-led growth, China pursued a policy of relative isolation. This exclusion from participation in the long boom of 1955–73 was the result of forces outside as well as within the PRC. In the context of the Cold War, the Communist-led PRC was isolated by American and United Nations embargoes on trade with China until the 1970s. After a political break with the USSR in 1960, China was cut off from Soviet capital and technology and the economy's growth capacity receded further. Partly on practical and partly on ideological grounds, Mao's regime turned to a policy of 'self-reliance' from the 1960s, seeking to industrialise by relying mainly on national resources of labour, natural resources and capital. On some measures, the self-reliance policy was successful since the share of industry in national income rose from about 13 per cent in 1949 to 47 per cent by 1980, but there were serious weaknesses in efficiency and technological capacity. In 1978, three quarters of the labour force was still engaged in the agricultural sector. The Great Leap Forward in 1960–2 attempted to rush heavy industrial expansion at the expense of agriculture and triggered one of the worst famines of the twentieth century. The Cultural Revolution launched in 1967 further enhanced the priority of ideology over economic progress until the early 1970s, sending a generation of urban dwellers to rural areas for re-education. During these decades, therefore, China remained fairly isolated from the rapid growth spurred by trade liberalisation in most of the developed world as it pursued a national economic policy that neglected consumption, employment creation and the service sector.

Mao launched his rapprochement with the United States in 1971 and met with a receptive mood in Washington. As well as the strategic advantages of engaging with the world's most populous nation, the Nixon administration was swayed by the potential gains for American companies if they won access to the huge Chinese market. A series of carefully orchestrated diplomatic exchanges culminated in the Shanghai Declaration in February 1973, which opened the way for the normalisation of trade relations between China and the United States and heralded a new chapter in China's international economic relations. After Mao's death in 1974, internal political division as well as the global economic maelstrom prompted by the first oil crisis disrupted the progress of reform. The political breakthrough was finally secured by Mao's successor, Deng Xiaoping, at the end of 1978 with the launch of the Open Door policy, which explicitly called for the use of foreign technology to improve industrial performance and the introduction of a limited range of market-orientated reforms in designated Special Economic Zones (SEZs) in China's eastern coastal regions. The rationale of the Open Door policy was to allow some producers to gain from the efficiency of engaging in markets but restricting this activity both by sector and region. In essence, the Chinese strategy was to try to combine socialist and market economics, by maintaining centralised state control over society and large parts of the economy, while reaping the benefits of a limited engagement with capitalism. Rather than an 'open door' to the global economy, the early process is actually better characterised as an 'open window' to reflect the limited scope and high obstacles to international economic engagement.

The first stage of the Open Door era lasted from 1979–85. In July 1979 four SEZs were established in Guangdong and Fujian provinces (Shenzhen, Shuhai, Shantou and Xiamen) where special policies were introduced to attract foreign capital and to promote exports, particularly from the Chinese diaspora in Taiwan and Hong Kong. The success of this first experiment prompted a further fourteen coastal port cities and Hainan Island to be opened to international trade and investment in 1984. Pent-up demand for capital goods and an overvalued currency prompted a surge of imports into China, causing a trade deficit until 1990. At first, exports were dominated by primary products and oil during the price boom of the early 1980s, while the manufacturing sector was progressively geared up for international competition by welcoming foreign firms. The first China-foreign joint venture, the Beijing Air Food Co., was launched in 1980. Over the next few years foreign investment trickled in, often frustrated by bureaucratic uncertainty and practical difficulties. Some of these obstacles were overcome by the October 1986 'Provisions for Encouragement of Foreign Investment', which specifically encouraged joint ventures between Chinese and foreign companies in technologically advanced enterprises and in export-orientated production. Foreign investors in these sectors were offered cheaper land and labour and easier access to foreign exchange. From 1985, exports of textiles and other light manufactures comprised a rising share of exports, so that manufactured goods amounted to over 75 per cent of total exports by 1991. Rather than the heavy industry of state-owned enterprises during the Mao era, these foreign joint ventures focused on labour-intensive production that exploited China's comparative advantage and so offered better prospects for gains from trade in terms of efficiency, as well as offering employment opportunities for the local population.

Trade and resource allocation remained state-controlled during the 1980s, and tariffs were used strategically to limit imports of consumer goods and favour imports of foreign technology and raw materials for manufacturing. The SEZ strategy was adapted from export processing zones initiated in a range of countries, such as that opened in 1966 at Kaohsiung in Taiwan, which helped drive that economy's successful industrialisation. This strategy aimed to control the influence of foreign capital geographically so as to limit competition with domestic producers and the domestic market. The goal was to earn foreign exchange, increase employment, attract foreign investment, accelerate technological and managerial innovation, and provide laboratories for economic reform, with the prospect that successful practices could eventually be extended to the rest of China. Table 5.3 shows the dramatic increase in the amount of FDI contracted with foreign companies and the amount that actually entered the economy each year. The combined result of the reforms was extraordinary per capita growth rates of almost 9 per cent p.a. in the 1980s.

Table 5.3 Foreign direct investment in China 1984–99 (US$ billion)

	Contracted	Utilised		Contracted	Utilised
1984	2.7	1.3	*1992*	58.1	11.0
1985	5.9	1.7	*1993*	111.4	27.5
1986	2.8	1.9	*1994*	82.7	33.8
1987	3.7	2.3	*1995*	91.3	37.5
1988	5.3	3.2	*1996*	73.3	41.7
1989	5.6	3.4	*1997*	51.0	45.3
1990	6.6	3.5	*1998*	52.1	45.5
1991	12.0	4.4	*1999*	41.2	40.4

Source: Chinability.com

In June 1989, the state's violent backlash against the nascent pro-democracy movement centred in Tiananmen Square threatened to de-rail China's re-emergence into the international economy. After a brief hiatus, however, foreign business confidence was quickly restored. Foreign investment was given a particular boost by Deng Xiaoping's 'Southern Tour' of the Xiamen region at the start of 1992, where he exhorted local governments to modernise at a faster pace. This was followed by the opening of twenty-eight cities and eight regions in the Yangtze River Delta area that convinced investors that the limits to political reform would not cause a reversal in the economic prospects for foreign firms. In 1992–3 alone, 132,000 companies with part-foreign participation were approved and US$170 billion worth of investment was contracted.

The path to modernisation was not easy or smooth. The weak legal framework for capitalist enterprise led to uncertainty for foreign companies that wanted to engage with the Chinese economy. Language and cultural differences presented further barriers for some investors from Japan and the West. The Joint Venture Law of 1979 set out the requirements for joint responsibility in foreign-invested enterprises, but there was a lack of local Chinese managerial experience to fulfil these requirements. Board membership tended to be politically awarded rather than on industrial or corporate experience. Legal restrictions and weak protection of property rights further undermined the attractions of investment through wholly foreign-owned enterprises until the 1990s. By the end of the decade, official data suggest that 30 per cent of foreign firms were making losses in China.

Partly by design, the bulk of foreign participation came from the Chinese diaspora in Taiwan and Hong Kong; the original SEZs were located in the traditional coastal home regions of these populations. The PRC's Open Door policy came at an opportune moment in the industrial expansion of several states in Asia where rising labour costs had all but exhausted the benefits to be gleaned from labour intensive production. By 1991 over a third of Hong Kong's manufacturing had been re-located to the Pearl River Delta in the neighbouring province of Guangdong to take advantage of relatively cheaper labour costs. Most Taiwanese investment was originally in the Xiamen area and was also dominated by labour-intensive manufacturing for export – mainly food processing and electronics. Until 1987 direct investment in the mainland was prohibited by the Taiwanese authorities, but entrepreneurs avidly pursued opportunities by channelling their investment through Hong Kong in the 1980s. Thus began an intensification of economic integration between the PRC, Taiwan and Hong Kong that accelerated through the 1990s in advance of the return of Hong Kong to Chinese sovereignty in 1997. While successful in generating employment and accumulations of foreign exchange, the technology and managerial transfer from these types of export-orientated assembly plants was fairly limited, and the Chinese government soon began to encourage higher value-added production. Japanese, European and American investment tended to be larger-scale production, located near major cities such as Shanghai and Beijing, often producing for the domestic market in industries such as automobile or mobile phone manufacture as well as services.

The re-emergence of the PRC into the international economy, although by no means complete or uncontested by 1990, contributed significantly to the breadth of the globalisation of international economic relations in this decade and captures some of the salient elements of this second globalisation: the emergence of less developed economies as major manufacturing exporters, the important role of international investment, the successful alleviation of absolute poverty, and the persistence of unequal distribution of income within and among countries.

Convergence and divergence

Did globalisation allow poorer countries to 'catch up' with the richer industrialised states? Ideally, more integrated markets could allow more countries to take part in wealth-enhancing international economic activity. Openness might lead to borrowing new ideas or innovations to increase productivity and might also create employment as demand for production reaches beyond the domestic market. The evidence on the causal relationship between liberalisation of trade and growth is somewhat mixed. Partly, this is because the income gains from trading alone are difficult to isolate from other factors such as geographical proximity to wealthy markets or the quality of local institutions, such as education.[10] During the 1980s, developing countries' real GDP grew slightly faster than developed countries (3.9 per cent vs. 3.2 per cent), but on a per capita basis, they grew slower (1.8 per cent vs. 2.5 per cent), suggesting falling relative living standards.[11] Only developing countries in East and Southeast Asia (including the PRC, Taiwan, South Korea and Singapore) achieved per capita growth rates higher than developed countries in this decade. This outcome partly reflects the evidence that in the 1980s and 1990s those countries that engaged more effectively with the international economy by reducing trade barriers and relaxing exchange controls did grow faster, and that poverty in these countries was reduced more than was the case for countries that pursued isolationist strategies. The big winners from globalisation in the 1990s (on a national rather than individual basis) were China, India, Mexico and Brazil where incomes per capita increased quickly as trade barriers were relaxed and production for export increased. The World Bank noted that in 1980 only a quarter of exports from developing economies were manufactures, but by 2000 this had reached over 80 per cent. Many countries in the developing world appeared to have escaped Raul Prebisch's structural bias against primary production that had plagued the 1960s and 1970s.

The World Bank sought to compare those countries where trade is most significant with those for which trade is a smaller share of GDP. It characterised the top third of developing countries in terms of share of trade in GDP as 'globalizers' on this measure and compared them to the rest of the developed world. Some of their results are in Table 5.4, which shows that while the 'globalizers' began in 1980 with lower per capita incomes, by 1997 they had increased incomes by two thirds compared with an increase of less than 10 per cent for other countries. Of course, not all the rise in income was due to increased exports or the liberalisation of trade. Underlying institutional reforms such as enhancing the rule of law, securing property rights, improving the local investment environment for foreign and domestic capital, creating good infrastructure and ensuring political stability are also crucial to development. Many of the poorest states with low ratios of trade to GDP were in sub-Saharan Africa where low levels of education and healthcare, civil war, dependence on primary product exports, insecure property rights and corruption have inhibited economic growth. While the causation between trade openness and growth is still hotly contested in the economics literature, engaging in world trade seems to be more related to higher incomes than a strategy of retreating from the international economy.

The relationship between growth and financial market liberalisation is even more highly contested than for merchandise trade.[12] Financial liberalisation itself, in the form of freeing up the domestic banking and investment system from tight regulations and allowing freer cross-border activity, should in theory have a positive impact on growth at least temporarily, but at the same time it makes an economy much more prone to crisis. We shall see that in the 1990s the sequencing of liberalisation without prior rigorous prudential supervision and sound governance structures made many

Table 5.4 World Bank analysis of gains to 'globalizers' 1980–97

	Top third: Trade/GDP ratio (24 states)	Bottom two thirds: Trade/ GDP ratio (49 states)
Population 1997	2.9 billion	1.1 billion
Per capita GDP 1980	US$1,488	US$1,947
Per capita GDP 1997	US$2,485	US$2,133
Inflation 1980 (% p.a.)	16	17
Inflation 1997 (% p.a.)	6	9

Source: World Bank, *Globalization, Growth and Poverty; Building an Inclusive World Economy*, 2002, p. 35

economies vulnerable to changes in investor sentiment. On the other hand, inward flows of investment can clearly be important in improving infrastructure, and for importing the technology and managerial skills that contribute to growth if the local conditions are right.

Along with the globalisation of production through trade and transnational corporations, global financial markets expanded quickly during the 1980s. Several factors contributed to rising activity in stock exchanges and other financial markets during this decade – including the liberalisation of restrictions on these markets, a rash of mergers and acquisitions among corporations, increased demand from new institutional investors such as pensions and mutual funds, and ICT innovations that made trading more swift and automatic. In 1987 the integration of global stock markets was starkly apparent as a crash in equity prices spread around the world. Share prices appear to have been overvalued in the exuberance of the market and a decline was triggered in mid-October 1987 by a range of factors, including a falling US dollar, higher interest rates and threats to tax breaks on company mergers in the United States. Once share prices began to tumble, automated trading systems prompted huge sales that further contributed to the crisis, culminating in a collapse known as Black Monday on 19 October. The Dow Jones Industrial Average stock index fell by its largest ever one-day decrease, dropping 507.99 to 1,738.74, or 22.6 per cent. The London FTSE fell by 11 per cent on Black Monday and 12 per cent the following day. The crisis was ended partly through the actions of regulators and central banks, which rushed to ensure liquidity in markets and reassure investors. The US Federal Reserve stated on Tuesday, 20 October that:

> The Federal Reserve, consistent with its responsibilities as the Nation's central bank, affirmed today its readiness to serve as a source of liquidity to support the economic and financial system.

As a result of the restoration of confidence and a resurgence in corporate merger activity, global stock markets recovered quickly from the 1987 crash, but the vulnerability of the international financial system to contagious crises in confidence had been clearly exposed. These weaknesses were to re-emerge in various guises during a series of currency and financial crises through the 1990s.

European monetary integration

As noted above, one of the factors contributing to the surge of international trade and investment from the mid-1980s was the further integration of the European economies. The fresh impetus toward the single market ran alongside further enlargement that changed the character of the EEC from its northwest Europe origins. The accession of Greece in 1981 and of Spain and Portugal in 1986 diversified the range of states within the customs union to include relatively lower income and more agricultural economies. This, in turn, presented new challenges for the EEC as it sought to promote the economic development of poorer regions and to bring these states into the CAP. In retrospect, it was this second wave of enlargement and the failure to achieve convergence among this more diverse group of countries that increased the vulnerability of the European integration project. Greece's inability to constrain its borrowing and weaknesses in the fiscal position of Spain and Portugal threatened to pull the euro apart in the spring of 2010.

The Exchange Rate Mechanism (ERM) launched in 1979 (see Chapter 4) evolved during the 1980s as countries joined and left. The constraints on national economic policies required in order to maintain the pegged rate system were substantial as unemployment and inflation rates periodically diverged, forcing countries to drop out of the system or to revalue their bilateral rates to the ECU. From 1979–87 there were eleven episodes of realignment of one or more currencies, comprising twenty-seven changes in parity, and a further seven realignments by 1995. The strength of the West German economy meant that the Deutschmark was appreciated in value seven times in the first ten years of the ERM, combining to a total of just over 25 per cent.[13] Nevertheless, there was considerable progress toward convergence to lower inflation among its members, as is shown in Table 5.5, which allowed the system to be considered a success. Inflation rates fell for many industrial countries in the 1980s, but those of ERM members fell faster and converged more.

By the end of the decade, however, various forces contributed to the erosion of the credibility of the system. The collapse of the Berlin Wall in 1989 and the subsequent reunification of East and West Germany weakened the anchor of the system as the German econom(ies) dealt with the

Table 5.5 Inflation rate convergence among ERM members 1975–89 (% p.a.)

	1975–8	1979–82	1983–6	1987	1988	1989
Average inflation rate	10.0	10.9	5.4	2.3	2.6	3.6
Standard deviation	3.7	4.9	2.5	1.9	1.6	1.5
Difference between highest and lowest	11.9	12.7	7.8	5.5	4.2	5.2
Coefficient of variation	37.3	44.6	47.4	80.9	63.6	41.8

Note: Coefficient of variation = (standard deviation/mean)*100.

Source: H. Ungerer *et al.*, *The European Monetary System: Developments and Perspectives*, IMF, Washington, 1990.

difficulties of integration. Another disruptive factor was the adoption of narrower exchange rate bands by Italy and the entry of sterling into the ERM for the first time in 1990. The lira had operated at a wider band of ±6 per cent around parity, which allowed greater flexibility within the system, but in January 1990 Italy adopted the stricter ±2.25 per cent band. Sterling joined with the wider band of ±6 per cent in October 1990. These two currencies would soon threaten the future of the ERM in the greatest crisis of its operation.

The Conservative government of Margaret Thatcher was particularly aggressive in its attempts to re-negotiate Britain's position in the EEC with respect to the UK's contribution to the EEC budget and was hostile to further erosion of national sovereignty. In 1979 the outgoing UK Labour government had opted not to join the ERM, preferring to retain sovereignty over the exchange rate as a tool of policy, and this position was extended by the incoming Thatcher government. The success of the ERM in apparently reducing inflation and promoting growth, however, gradually led to a change of policy within the Conservative government of the 1980s. By 1989 Thatcher was ready to adopt the policy constraints of the ERM and sterling joined in October 1990. Unfortunately, this timing was ill-favoured by a recession and falling property prices. Although UK inflation did converge toward the lower European average, sterling's ERM exchange rate was ultimately unsustainable.

In the midst of Britain's struggles in the ERM, progress toward EMU was being pursued in Brussels. In 1984, Jacques Delors, President of the European Commission, issued a White Paper on the Internal Market as a blueprint to build the next stage of economic integration through a single market. Although tariffs had been eliminated in trade among member states, other barriers such as institutional and regulatory differences continued to hamper economic exchange. In 1986 the Commission adopted the Single European Act to eliminate these barriers and move the EEC from a customs union to a single market in goods, people and capital within six years. This was the first major revision of the Treaty of Rome and increased the power and flexibility of European political institutions to help streamline the integration process. Despite the existence of the ERM to stabilise exchange rates, periodic revaluations and price support meant that in 1985, the CAP absorbed over 70 per cent of the EC budget, giving rise to further pressure to find a way to stabilise exchange rates more permanently.

The 1989 Delors Report of the Special Committee on Monetary Union set out the prospects for returning to the Werner Report's plans for EMU, which had been abandoned in the early 1970s. With agreement to a single market already concluded, the Committee set out the requirements for a complete monetary unification; common currency, single central bank, single monetary policy and fiscal co-ordination. The report was widely debated and generated particular animosity in the UK, where part of the population had deep misgivings over the amount of sovereignty already lost to European institutions.

Delors' vision for EMU to be achieved by 1999 was finally approved at the Maastricht summit in December 1991, and the treaty was ratified by member governments during the following year. The goal of EMU required gradual convergence of EC economies, including convergence targets for fiscal deficits: no more than 3 per cent of GDP and public debt of no more than 60 per cent of GDP, and inflation within 1.5 per cent of the three lowest-inflation EC states. Just as the terms were being ratified, however, turmoil in the ERM threatened its prospects.

During the summer of 1992 a crisis of confidence in the future of the sterling and lira exchange rates accumulated. In the UK, rising unemployment and poor housing returns appeared to be evidence of a weakened economy while the lira also struggled within its narrow band. In August, the German central bank made clear that it was unwilling to relax German interest rates in order to relieve pressure on the weakest currencies in the ERM framework. In mid-September the Italian lira was devalued by 7 per cent, causing tremendous speculation to spread against the pound as financiers expected sterling also to fall in value. The Bank of England sought to sustain its value for several weeks by selling US$40 billion of foreign exchange and raising interest rates, but on 16 September 1992 the pound was forced to float free of the ERM parity. The lesson drawn from this costly and humiliating experience by a generation of British voters and policy-makers was that the potential cost of exchange rate stability within common European institutions was not worth the ultimate benefit. Subsequent British governments have remained hostile to joining in monetary union with the rest of Europe.

Conclusions and summary

After the turmoil of the 1970s and the debt crisis of the early 1980s, the world entered an era of globalisation as trade, migration and capital flows expanded quickly and more countries were engaged more intensively in international economic relations. The greater integration of the world economy arose both from regional policies such as European integration and from political changes that affected barriers among individual states, such as the end of the Maoist era in China and the collapse of the Soviet Union in 1991. As a prevailing liberal economic ideology took hold and communications innovation accelerated, the liberalisation of trade that begun in the 1960s was reinforced by freer capital and financial flows. By the mid-1990s it seemed that the tenets of neo-classical economics had been proved right by the dramatic economic success of many developing countries that engaged in international trade and investment, even though these policies were often state-directed rather than left to market forces. In fact, however, the world was on the brink of another set of crises that would rock the foundations of the liberal agenda.

6 The acceleration of globalisation and renewed crises 1995–9

During the 1990s, globalisation accelerated as trade and financial liberalisation spread beyond the rich industrial states to emerging markets. This process was enhanced by the reduction in political barriers to international economic relations. The collapse of the Berlin Wall in 1989 and the break-up of the Soviet Union in 1991 heralded the creation of more market-orientated states in Eastern Europe and the prospect for further enlargement of the European Community. In China and India, market-orientated reforms embedded these economies into the international system. Further innovation in communications and information technology prompted fresh surges of investment, trade and international migration. In the process, however, the vulnerability of global markets to contagion was exposed in a series of currency and banking crises that spread from emerging markets. By the end of the decade, debate raged over the purpose of core international economic institutions such as the IMF, and states increasingly used institutions of regional co-operation to reform the architecture of the international economic system.

Spread of global economic activity

During the 1990s there was a geographical redistribution of international economic activity as several emerging markets increased their manufacturing exports, but the poorest states continued to be left behind. The share of world exports held by UNCTAD's category of developing countries (excluding China) rose from 22 per cent to 28 per cent, mainly at the expense of the EU (whose share of world exports fell from 44 per cent to 40 per cent) and Japan (whose share fell from 8 per cent to 7 per cent). However, the poorest developing countries did not increase their share of world trade at all, and the share of world exports held by the African least-developed countries (LDCs) actually fell from 0.5 per cent to 0.3 per cent. Figure 6.1 shows that in the 1990s developing countries recovered some of the fall in their share of FDI flows that had characterised the 1980s, but this share still remained below 30 per cent of the world total. An exception was the rise in China as a target for FDI, which is discussed below. The LDCs continued to receive less than 1 per cent of world FDI flows during the 1980s and 1990s, and the share of African developing countries (excluding South Africa) actually fell from 2.5 per cent in the 1980s to 1.7 per cent on average in the 1990s. Outward flows of FDI from developing countries increased from about 5 per cent of the world total in the 1980s to 11 per cent in the 1990s, but about a third of this total was Hong Kong investment in mainland China. It appears that the problem of unequal participation of the poorest countries in the international economy continued, although Chapter 5 showed that globalisation provided opportunities for many developing economies to raise their relative incomes.

International economic relations were profoundly affected by the boundary changes that followed the end of the Cold War in Europe. During the 1990s, fresh states were created from the collapse of the Soviet Union, the separation of the Czech and Slovak republics and the Balkan wars in Yugoslavia. In each case, new national currencies and trading apparatuses were instituted, and Chapter 5 has shown that there was renewed migration across the borders of the new states. The process of amalgamating East and West Germany slowed the German engine of the European economy, but the benefits of opening markets to fast growing European states attracted Finland, Sweden and Austria to join the European Union (EU) in 1995. With the accelerating pace of monetary and economic union, the opportunity costs of remaining outside the EU were rising. Accession to the EU was an important goal for many East and Central European states as part of their transition to market economies and in an effort to promote prosperity for their populations and legitimacy for their regimes. During the 1990s, this impetus prompted negotiations for a new round of enlargement that brought the total number of members from sixteen to twenty-six in 2004.[1] This expansion eastward was followed in 2007 by the accession of Romania and Bulgaria. The economic implications of this expansion will be considered in Chapter 7.

As well as trade, migration and investment, the acceleration of globalisation in financial markets was dramatic in the 1990s. Figure 6.2 shows that banks were becoming increasingly international in their activities so that the share of external assets in total assets grew steadily in the 1990s. About 60–70 per cent of these external assets were loans and advances between banks rather than claims on non-banks, reflecting a rise in financial activity such as speculative forward positions or security derivatives, which might be considered distant from the real economic activity on which they were based. This trend was to have dramatic consequences in the international financial crisis of 2007–8.

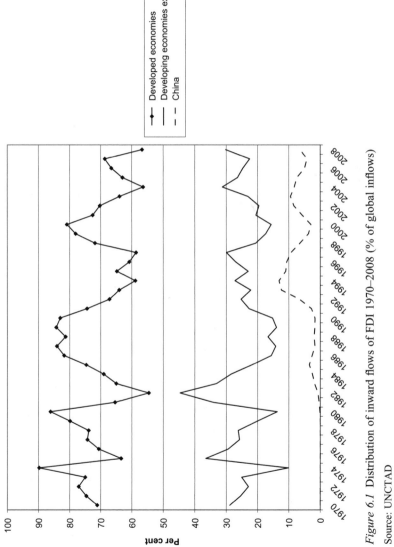

Figure 6.1 Distribution of inward flows of FDI 1970–2008 (% of global inflows)

Source: UNCTAD

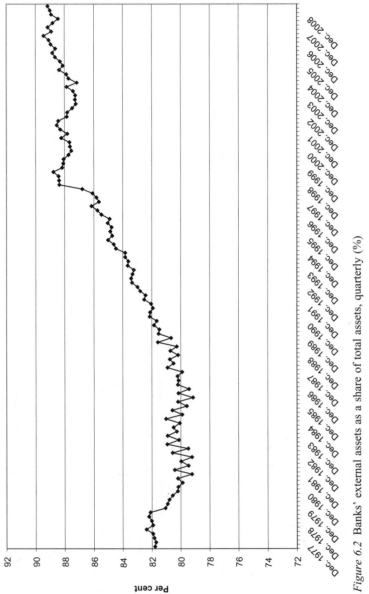

Figure 6.2 Banks' external assets as a share of total assets, quarterly (%)

Source: BIS

The geographical distribution of foreign bank assets shifted markedly toward Europe. European banks held about one third of the total in 1983 and close to 60 per cent by the end of the 1990s, rising to 70 per cent by 2005. Just over half of these foreign assets were loans and advances to borrowers in other developed European countries. The internationalisation of global banking was thus tied to the growth and integration of the European market. Banks in the United States, by contrast, accounted for only 10 per cent of global foreign bank assets in 2005.

Equity markets also surged ahead from 1995–2000, driven by new venture companies that promised to generate huge profits from exploiting the World Wide Web (WWW) and by a growing hunger for equity investments from institutions such as mutual funds, insurance companies and pension schemes. The potential for gains from the commercial opportunities of the WWW favoured small start-up companies that sought to gain large market share quickly by reaching a global customer base, but many were caught by difficult logistics of sourcing and delivering products to extremely broad geographical areas or failing to develop models that effectively captured payments for viewing content. Figure 6.3 shows the surge in New York's NASDAQ composite index, peaking on 10 March 2000, a day when 2 billion shares were traded. Higher interest rates, poor financial results from the Christmas third quarter, and a legal case against market-leader Microsoft all contributed to a change in market sentiment that abruptly prompted sales of shares as investors expected prices to fall. Once prices slipped, more investors tried to liquidate their portfolios and share values tumbled. As the exuberance in the market evaporated, a series of bankruptcies further shook the American business scene, including Enron, the seventh-largest company in the United States, which entered the broadband market in 2000, and Worldcom, America's third-largest telecommunications company. The accounting fraud that lay behind the spectacular growth and confidence in these companies prompted fresh calls for more oversight from regulators to protect investors and employees.

The dot.com crash affected US economic performance by shaking business confidence and investment and contributing to unemployment. These effects were reinforced by the attack on the Twin Towers in New York on 11 September 2001, which shook the core of the capitalist system and drew the United States into costly wars in Afghanistan and Iraq. The growth of the US economy fell from about 4 per cent p.a. in the years from 1996 to 2000 to only 1 per cent in 2001. In this uncertain environment a renewed challenge to American economic dominance appeared in East and Southeast Asia.

It is clear from the trade and investment data presented above that a key driver of the redistribution of global economic activity in the 1990s was

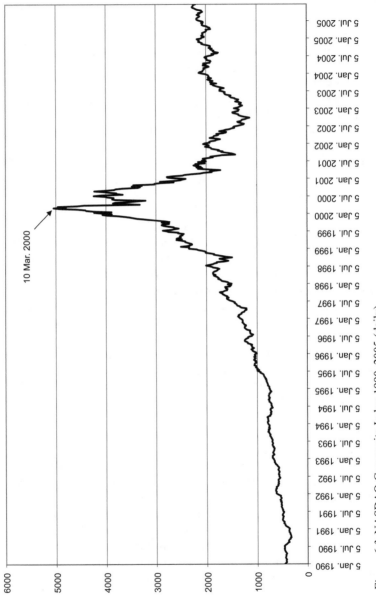

Figure 6.3 NASDAQ Composite Index 1990–2005 (daily)

Source: Yahoo Finance

the continued economic rise of China. Chapter 5 showed how China's engagement with the international economy accelerated after the mid-1980s. Over the next two decades, China's economic growth continued to be boosted by massive inflows of foreign direct investment as companies from around the world sought to take advantage of cheaper production costs (especially low wages) and the huge and increasingly wealthy market for consumer goods and services in China. Chapter 5 also showed that annual inflows of foreign direct investment rose from US$3.5 billion to over $40 billion from 1990 to 1999. In the 1980s China absorbed less than 2 per cent of world FDI, but in the 1990s on average over 7 per cent of FDI flowed to China. According to UNCTAD, China also increased its share of world trade, accounting for 1.8 per cent of world exports in 1990 and 3.8 per cent by 2000, representing a nominal increase in exports from US$62 million to $249 million. The pace of exports greatly exceeded imports, so that China's trade surplus grew from US$4 billion in 1992 to $29 billion by 1999. Trade and foreign investment were closely related, partly because cheap labour and low environmental costs attracted foreign factories to China to process or assemble goods for export. In 1990, firms with foreign participation accounted for about 13 per cent of exports from China and less than 3 per cent of overall industrial production, but by 2000 foreign firms' share of exports had risen to 48 per cent and the share of industrial production was 27 per cent. With the yuan pegged to the US dollar in 1994, the combination of trade surplus and large net inflows of investment led to an accumulation of reserves from US$20.6 billion in 1992 to $146 billion by 1999. This accumulation set the scene for intense trade friction and controversy over China's exchange rate policy, which will be considered in Chapter 7.

China's presence in international markets was reinforced by increased participation in multilateral economic institutions. China joined the World Bank in 1980 and by 1993 was the largest single recipient of support from this organisation (although ranking much lower in per capita terms). Figure 6.4 shows that after a hiatus in lending after the Tiananmen Square incident in 1989, the pace of lending from the International Bank for Reconstruction and Development accelerated throughout the 1990s. From July 1999 China became too wealthy to qualify for the softest form of aid, from the World Bank's International Development Agency arm, but it continued to benefit from other forms of support, albeit at a reduced rate during the 2000s. By 2010, China had received US$37.6 billion in support from World Bank projects, about half of which was directed toward agriculture, water sanitation and transport projects that aimed to alleviate poverty and redress the increasingly unequal distribution of income between rural and urban populations and between provinces in the east compared with those in central and western regions. Sustained high rates of economic growth in the 1990s

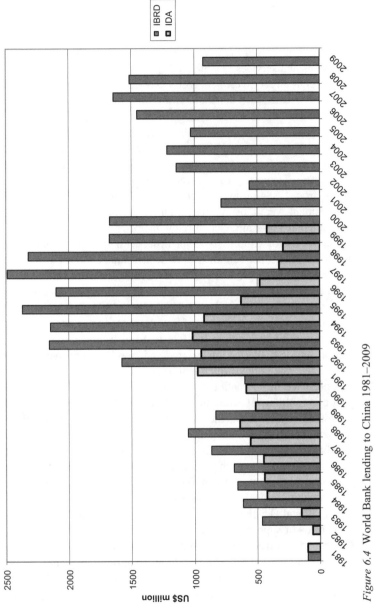

Figure 6.4 World Bank lending to China 1981–2009

Source: World Bank

allowed most of China's population to escape from poverty, so that by 2005 less than 3 per cent of Chinese fell below the poverty line defined by the Chinese government. Still, according to the World Bank over a third of Chinese survived on less than the equivalent of US$2 per day. The richest 10 per cent of the population shared almost a third of China's total income, while the poorest 10 per cent shared less than 3 per cent.

In 1986 China applied to join the GATT, but the progress of negotiations was quickly bogged down by mismatched expectations and little progress was made until the mid-1990s, when the WTO was established. During the process of WTO accession, the relationship with the United States was crucial since a bilateral agreement with the world's largest economy was required before a complete set of trade agreements with all WTO members could be signed. During the 1990s the US trade deficit with China grew from US$10 billion to $69 billion, and this imbalance became a key obstacle in the negotiations. Although imports of cheap, labour-intensive consumer goods may have reduced the cost of living for Americans, the growing imbalance prompted protectionist calls from US politicians, who viewed these imports as a threat to American jobs. In response to protectionist lobbies, both the EU and the United States made repeated recourse to quota restrictions on Chinese goods, such as clothing. A further obstacle to accession was the need to conform China's legal structures to the WTO's new rules protecting intellectual property (IP). The prevalence of media piracy and illegal copying of technology was a particular barrier to trade between the United States and China; American exports tended to have a high IP content so producers were reluctant to sell to China and risk having their product copied. Cheap fakes also squeezed out legitimate goods from the market. Without WTO membership, China's trade with the United States was subjected to annual reviews in the US Congress where human rights and political issues were raised that added friction to Sino-American relations. Given the increasing resistance to inexpensive Chinese products in a range of developed markets, WTO membership offered China the prospect of more stable trading relations and an outside arbiter to settle disputes. While progress toward China's accession to the WTO faced obstacles from trading partners, there was also internal dissention over the process.

More open markets threatened social unrest and challenges to the political status quo in both urban and rural sectors of China. Freer trade in agricultural products threatened the incomes of the 70 per cent of China's population that still lived in rural areas in the 1990s. International competition also threatened inefficient state-owned enterprises (SOEs) in the industrial sector. Reforming the SOEs either through restructuring or closure required some transitional unemployment that could only be resolved by allowing more labour mobility throughout China and relaxation of state controls. Many social services had traditionally been distributed through SOEs, so restructuring also implied an increased central fiscal responsibility for social welfare. A third problematic area was the WTO requirement to allow greater competition in finance and banking, at a time when the state-owned banking system was weakened by a legacy of large amounts of state-induced loans to SOEs that had little prospect of being repaid. Resolving this so-called 'non-performing loan' problem and thereby improving national banks' balance sheets was a prerequisite to allowing greater competition from foreign banks. On the other hand, for reformers within China, accession to the WTO offered the attractions of an external commitment mechanism to continue market-orientated policies. Once China had joined the WTO and acceded to its rules and dispute mechanism, the process of economic liberalisation would be much more difficult for domestic conservative forces to reverse.

As part of the process of accession, China reduced its tariff protection from about 43 per cent on average in 1992 to an average of 17 per cent by the end of 1997. However, much higher rates prevailed for some products, such as automobiles and rice, and trade was hindered by non-tariff barriers such as administrative controls and quotas. After a series of difficult negotiations between Chinese President Jiang Zemin and US President Bill Clinton during 1999, a bilateral trade agreement was finally agreed in November 1999 to allow progress for China's accession at the Seattle WTO meeting that month. In the Sino-US trade agreement China agreed to reduce agricultural tariffs still further to an average of 15 per cent and to reduce industrial tariff protection to an average of 9.4 per cent by 2005. Still, disputes over China's status as a developing economy in the WTO and protection for its agricultural sector continued to pose difficulties. Moreover, the Seattle WTO conference was disrupted by violent anti-globalisation demonstrations and China's accession was further delayed. The US Congress reluctantly voted to accord China Permanent Normal Trading Relations status in May 2000 and this was confirmed by the US Senate in September, thus eliminating the need for annual reviews of US policy. With bilateral Sino-US relations on a more stable footing, the path was open for China to sign agreements with other members to achieve final accession to the WTO. During 2001, the terms of the accession were finalised, including non-discriminatory treatment of all WTO members and freer trade in a range goods and services to be phased in over three to five years. China reserved state trading for key strategic products such as grain and tobacco and relatively high tariffs on some products such as motorcycles (45 per cent), cars (25 per cent), rice (65 per cent) and sugar (50 per cent). The final accession document was signed in December 2001 ushering in a new phase of China's international economic relations, and coinciding with a renewed surge in China's balance-of-payments surplus.

While the Chinese economy boomed during the 1990s, Japan as the traditional powerhouse of Asia fell into a prolonged period of slow growth, known as the 'Lost Decade'. Asset market booms in the late 1980s, particularly in real estate and equity shares, came to an abrupt end in 1990, causing a financial crisis as well as exposing corruption between the industrial and political establishment. During the years that followed, consumer confidence remained at a low level and investment rates ebbed. These two traditional drivers of Japan's dramatic economic success from the 1960s to the 1980s appeared to have become dislocated from the growth process, and even a rapid reduction in interest rates from 6 per cent in 1990 to 0.5 per cent by 1996 could not promote investment and consumption. The economy grew on average only about 1.0 per cent per year from 1992–2000 compared to 3.7 per cent p.a. in the 1980s (real GDP p.a., according to UNCTAD figures), and inflation turned negative so that prices were falling on average from 1992 to 1997. The resulting slowdown in Japan's absorption of its neighbouring economies' production (trade fell from 24 per cent of Japanese GDP in the 1980s to 18 per cent in the 1990s, and developing Asia's share of Japan's imports fell from 49 per cent to 45 per cent) weakened the fabric of the regional trading system in Asia and contributed to the fragility underlying the Asian financial crisis of 1997, which is discussed below.

International economic co-operation

As noted in previous chapters, the process of trade liberalisation benefited rich industrial countries as barriers were quickly reduced on the exchange of manufactured goods. On the other hand, developing countries and, in particular, agricultural producers continued to face substantial barriers to their exports as rich countries protected their domestic farmers through high tariff and non-tariff barriers. This distortion of the achievements of the GATT was recognised in the 1980s, but it took several years for members to agree to make a concerted effort to overcome this bias against agricultural producers. The Uruguay Round of the GATT was launched in 1986 to target reducing tariffs in outstanding areas such as trade in services, agriculture and textiles and to raise standards of intellectual property rights (IPR). The following years saw successful reforms of the disputes settlement system and monitoring of trade practices, but the issue of liberalising agricultural trade failed to make progress. Strong political lobbies in industrialised countries blocked freer trade in competing temperate and sub-tropical products so that the trade concessions in 1988 were limited to tropical products. As deadlines passed without progress, the Uruguay Round negotiations appeared to be failing and the focus of negotiations turned to areas where some agreement seemed possible – on rules for IPR, anti-dumping regulations and planning for a new apparatus to replace the GATT. Finally, in April 1994 an agreement was signed by the 123 member states to reform the GATT and set a timetable to re-open negotiations on IPR and trade in services and agriculture. Freer trade in services such as telecommunications and finance, which were of greater benefit to richer nations, were quickly completed by 1997. Negotiations on agriculture, on the other hand, were scheduled to start much later, in 2000, and subsequently became part of the Doha Development Agenda.

The focus on agriculture was overtaken by the plans to supersede the GATT with a new and more comprehensive institution, the World Trade Organisation, which was established in Geneva in January 1995 as part of the reforms of the Uruguay Round. As noted in Chapter 2, the world's governments had failed to ratify an International Trade Organisation in 1947, so it might be claimed that the WTO was forty-eight years in the making. In the meantime, the considerable advances in trade liberalisation under the GATT made it easier for states to accept a more formal institution with an elaborate monitoring and dispute settlement framework. On the one hand, freer global trade in manufactures by the 1990s (compared with 1946) meant that there was less scope for significant infringement on the national sovereignty of the wealthy leading nations, while on the other hand, the WTO promised to protect their access to international markets. Meanwhile, the existing rules allowed for continued protection of agricultural producers. For its first five years, the WTO concentrated on implementing the Uruguay Round General Agreements on Trade in Goods (GATG), the General Agreement on Trade in Services (GATS) and on trade-related aspects of intellectual property rights (TRIPS). These were the three main pillars of the WTO, underpinned by a system for countries to bring trade disputes to the WTO for legal settlement and enforcement.

Progress was made in the first years of the WTO on some of the goals identified in the Uruguay Round. Tariffs on trade of industrial products were further reduced by developed countries from an average of 6.3 per cent to 3.8 per cent by the end of the decade, and there was special focus on ensuring freer trade in information technology. The Uruguay Round had committed developed countries to reduce their tariffs and export subsidies in agriculture by 36 per cent by 2000. Developing countries had ten years (until 2005) to reduce their tariffs and subsidies on agricultural trade by 24 per cent, although the poorest nations were exempted. Some exceptions were allowed in cases where freer trade threatened sensitive food areas; for example Japan, the Philippines and South Korea continued to protect their rice producers.

Further progress on general agricultural trade liberalisation and promoting the interests of developing countries proved difficult.

At the 2001 WTO meeting in Qatar, members agreed to a Doha Development Agenda, but subsequent meetings in Cancun (2003) and Hong Kong (2005) were marred by conflict over agricultural trade and disappointment among developing economies over the commitment of rich nations to meaningful reform. The public's faith in the ability of the WTO and other multilateral institutions to deliver equitable and tangible outcomes was at a low ebb, particularly after the economic upheaval of the 1990s, which will be discussed below. In July 2006, as the prospect for agreement evaporated, the Doha negotiations were suspended. In order to renew progress, a more decentralised system of working groups was established in November 2006 to try to break through the impasse. WTO Director-General Pascal Lamy remarked at this time that:

> All the ships in our convoy have been in dry dock for repairs over the last few weeks. We are obviously not going to push them back into the water without preparing them adequately beforehand. This also requires the ship-owners to give the right sort of orders to their crews. You can rely on me to keep on pressing them to do so.[2]

The renewed negotiations finally delivered some consensus in July 2008, which led to final drafts for agreement on how tariffs and subsidies would be reduced, although without binding any country to accepting these targets. Unfortunately, the global financial crisis struck just as this meeting was concluded and although progress was made on finalising the draft suggestions by December 2008, little tangible progress could yet be claimed.

There are evident benefits of free international trade for growth, but the difficulties of achieving this on a global platform prompted the negotiation of a series of free trade agreements among regional partners. Enduring examples developed in this decade include Mercosur in 1991 (among Argentina, Brazil, Paraguay and Uruguay) and the ASEAN free trade area the following year (comprising Brunei, Indonesia, Malaysia, the Philippines, Singapore and Thailand). Among the largest regional trading groups in terms of volume of trade was the North American Free Trade Area (NAFTA), signed at the beginning of 1994 by the United States, Canada and Mexico. Discussion began formally in 1991 after it was decided to extend a proposed bilateral US–Canada free trade area to Mexico. The negotiations were prolonged and difficult, with the balance of power between the United States and two much smaller economies provoking distrust and fears that the United States would dominate any joint organisation. Nevertheless, the size of the US market and the importance of open access across the border was a powerful incentive for these countries to conclude NAFTA. While the huge American economy was the largest trading partner for both Canada and Mexico, Canada was also the USA's largest trading partner and Mexico was its third-largest partner. Figure 6.5 shows that Mexico and Canada relied heavily on trade within the NAFTA countries from the 1980s, almost all of which was bilateral trade with the United States. The 1994 agreement was thus signed after a decade of increasing reliance on the US market for these countries. This trend continued for a while after NAFTA was signed but then receded from 2001, mainly due to the rise of China as a global trading presence and liberalisation of trade with the rest of the world. A similar pattern of increasing trade intensity was seen for the United States with its NAFTA partners, but at a lower level. Isolating the effect of the trade agreement from other changes in the national and international economic environment is difficult, but the impact on trade has been slightly positive particularly across the Mexico–United States border and the impact on output and productivity in Mexico may also have been positive, partly through increased FDI.[3]

The NAFTA treaty established a timetable for the gradual reduction of trade barriers over fifteen years, concluding in 2008, although most progress was achieved before this date. By the end of 1994, Mexico had eliminated tariffs on about half of industrial imports from the United States and most Canada–US trade was tariff free by 1998. Some exceptions were allowed, including Canadian controls on exports of logs and fish, and special considerations were included for the cross-border automotive and television industries. NAFTA also extended to trade in services and cross-border investment, although tight legal restrictions persist on movement of people among the three states, and in the case of the US–Mexico border a physical wall was constructed. Despite these obstacles to flows of labour, the American economy arguably became even more dependent on legal and illegal immigrant workers from Mexico in the 1990s. NAFTA has governed a rising volume of trade among the three states and an increasing US trade deficit with these partners.

Financial crises in emerging markets

During the 1990s and into the early years of the new millennium, there was a series of exchange rate crises in emerging markets: in Mexico, Asia, Russia and Argentina. These crises shared similar characteristics, although all had local triggers. During the run-up to the crises governments liberalised markets, pegged exchange rates to the US dollar and enjoyed large inward capital flows generated by optimism over their economic growth potential. They tended to run current account deficits and their currencies gradually

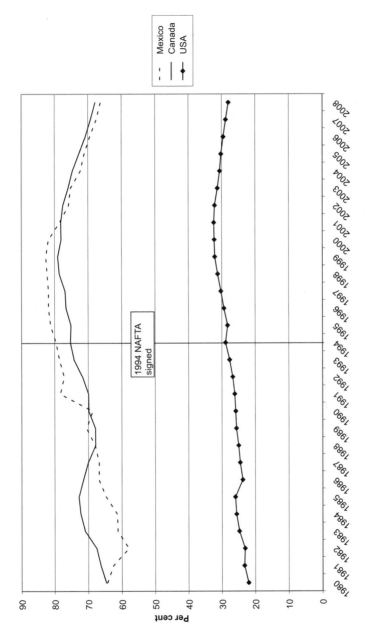

Figure 6.5 Share of NAFTA partners in each member's total trade 1980–2008 (%)

Source: Direction of Trade Statistics, 2010

became overvalued. Sudden shifts in confidence led to sharp reversals of capital flows that prompted exchange rate crises, with dramatic effects on the real economy. The IMF was then called in to provide emergency finance to stem currency freefall and restore confidence in these states' ability to repay debt and correct their balance-of-payments problems. In return, governments had to commit to a range of policies to restore current account balance, contain inflation and reduce government borrowing. Not all of the pledged support was actually drawn (in the case of Indonesia and South Korea, for example, the 'second line' of defence pledged by national governments was not used), but the headline amounts offered were needed to restore confidence. After the end of the immediate financial crisis, economic recession often spread to neighbouring economies, with few countries escaping even if their economic fundamentals had been sound before the crisis broke. Table 6.1 shows the dynamic changes in the volume of output in a range of affected countries, highlighting the pattern of recession from Mexico in 1995 to Argentina in 2002, as well as the rapid recovery in most cases.

After each successive case there was considerable public commentary and debate that emphasised the need to learn lessons from these episodes in order to avoid similar crises elsewhere by reforming the international financial 'architecture'.[4] One feature of this analysis was a critique of the sequence of opening capital markets before there was a sound governance structure in the domestic financial system. Prudential supervision and transparent governance of banks was needed to ensure the quality of borrowing and the robustness of financial systems to sudden reversals. As a result, the emphasis of policy reform shifted from relaxing capital controls to improving national supervisory systems to ensure prudent borrowing and lending. On the global scale, the rules established after the 1982 Latin American debt crisis by the Bank for International Settlements (Basel I),

Table 6.1 Annual per cent change in GDP volume for a range of emerging market economies 1994–2003

	1994	1995	1996	1997	1998	1999	2000	2001	2002	2003
Mexico	4.4	−6.2	5.2	6.8	5.0	3.8	6.6	0.0	0.8	1.4
Thailand	9.0	9.2	5.9	−1.4	−10.5	4.4	4.8	2.2	5.3	7.0
Indonesia	7.5	8.2	7.8	4.7	−13.1	0.8	4.9	3.6	4.5	4.8
South Korea	8.5	9.2	7.0	4.7	−6.9	9.5	8.5	4.0	7.2	2.8
Malaysia	9.2	9.8	10.0	7.3	−7.4	6.1	8.9	0.5	5.4	5.8
Russian Federation	–	–	−3.6	1.4	−5.3	5.1	10.5	5.1	4.7	8.2
Argentina	5.8	−2.8	5.5	8.1	3.9	−3.4	−0.8	−4.4	−10.9	8.8

Source: IMF, *International Financial Statistics*

which were aimed at sovereign debt risk, were shown to be inadequate to forestall the causes of the 1990s crises, which arose often from flows of capital into private banks and asset markets. The Basel Accord was duly revised (Basel II) to include rules for the minimum capital to be held by banks against a broader range of lending to the private sector, which was agreed in 2004. Again, as in the 1990s, the rules were gradually adopted and states had begun to implement them just as a further global financial crisis struck, this time in 2007–8. In the meantime, the financial crises of the 1990s posed a large burden on the populations of a range of middle-income economies.

The signing of NAFTA at the beginning of 1994 promised a bright future for the Mexican economy as it was linked more closely to its rich neighbour, and the prospects for further industrial development appeared bright. The Mexican government seemed committed to the liberal reforms promoted by the IMF and supported by the global financial community, including trade and market liberalisation, privatisation of industry and banks, monetary and fiscal restraint anchored by a banded pegged exchange rate to the US dollar and a pact between the state and labour unions to contain wage inflation. These policies were designed to deliver growth outcomes similar to the Asian economic 'miracles' of the 1980s. By the end of the year, however, the Mexican peso had collapsed and the IMF was drawn into a substantial support package.

The causes of the Peso Crisis of December 1994 were partly political and partly economic. From 1991 Mexico had been running a growing trade deficit that resulted in a current account deficit amounting to almost 7 per cent of GDP in the third quarter of 1993. This deficit was financed by substantial short-term borrowing mainly from foreign private lenders through sales of short-term government debt and inflows into the stock market and banks. From 1990 to 1994 about US$100 billion of private capital flowed into Mexico, about one quarter of which was foreign direct investment, one quarter in the stock market and about half in purchases of short-term government bonds.[5] Although inflation was falling, the peso was clearly overvalued, making some kind of devaluation inevitable. When the Zapatista movement assassinated presidential candidate Luis Donaldo Colosio on 23 March 1994, inflows of capital dried up while the current account balance continued to deteriorate. In September the Chief Executive of the ruling PRI party, Ruiz Massieu, was also assassinated, further shocking global confidence in the government. Reserves were run down from US$29 billion in February 1994 to only US$6 billion by the end of the year to sustain the exchange rate.[6] After a renewed run on reserves in November the peso was devalued 15 per cent on 20 December, but the market quickly forced the peso into freefall the next day. By March 1995 the exchange rate had fallen by 98 per cent, the share price index had fallen 28 per cent and interest rates rose to over 80 per cent p.a. The resulting contraction of lending and fragility in the banking system provoked a severe recession in Mexico through 1995, when GDP fell 6 per cent in real terms.

The collapse of the peso quickly affected other emerging market currencies as investors took cover by withdrawing their lending, in a process known as the 'Tequila Effect'. Argentina and other Latin American countries were particularly hard hit as capital fled their financial systems, interest rates had to be increased and domestic economic activity was repressed. The danger of systemic crisis drew the United States and multilateral lenders in to rescue the Mexican situation through short-term loans – better to bail out one economy than allow the crisis to spread. In exchange for agreeing to a harsh stabilisation plan, by February 1995 Mexico had negotiated a US$17.8 billion short-term loan from the IMF and $20 billion in short-term lending and guarantees from the US Exchange Stabilisation Fund. A further US$14 billion in credit was arranged with the government of Canada, the World Bank, and the Inter-American Development Bank.[7] The result was a relatively swift recovery by 1996, but the fragility of investors' confidence in emerging markets and the dangers of moral hazard from potential bailouts had longer-term consequences.

Two years later, a similar but more widespread crisis struck Southeast and East Asia with particularly severe effects in Thailand, Indonesia and South Korea. These countries had shared in the East Asian economic miracle, and were much praised by the World Bank for their liberal economic reforms and outward-looking export-led growth strategies. After liberalising their capital markets, they attracted substantial inflows of foreign investment that sustained current account deficits and led to booming property and stock markets in the region. For example, net capital inflows into Thailand, where the crisis began, amounted to 10 per cent of GDP from 1990–6. Most currencies in the region were pegged to the US dollar, which began to appreciate in 1995, leading to overvaluation and further weakening the balance of payments in many Asian countries. Slow growth in the Japanese economy, formerly the regional engine of economic growth, and the depreciation of the Chinese yuan in 1994 added to challenges in regional export markets.

The crisis began in Thailand in July 1997 with the collapse of the Thai baht after evidence of a mounting balance-of-payments deficit and falling reserves destroyed confidence in the state's ability to defend the parity against the US dollar. The exchange rate was allowed to sink from 2 July and had lost one fifth of its value in terms of the US dollar by the end of the month. In August, a support package totalling about US$17 billion was arranged to restore confidence and liquidity (see Table 6.2). By this time,

Table 6.2 Crisis support (approximate amounts offered) (US$ billion)

	Mexico	Thailand	Indonesia	South Korea
IMF	17.8	4.0	10.1	21.1
World Bank/Asian Development Bank		2.7	8.0	14.2
Co-ordinated bilateral government support	34.0	10.5	18.0	23.1
Total	41.8	17.2	36.1	58.4
Total as % of GDP	15	12	17	13

Source: T. Lane, A. Ghosh, J. Hamann, S. Phillips, M. Schulze-Ghattas and T. Tsikata, *IMF-Supported Programs in Indonesia, Korea, and Thailand: A Preliminary Assessment*, Occasional Paper 178, IMF, 1999 (Mexico data from author's calculations)

however, a contagion effect on international investor confidence had spread to other newly industrialising economies in the region, and as capital was withdrawn the weaknesses in the domestic financial systems in many countries were exposed. In November, after the rupiah had lost about a third of its value against the US dollar, Indonesia arranged US$36 billion in financial support from the IMF, World Bank, Asian Development Bank and various governments. After increasing by 4.7 per cent in 1997, the volume of Indonesian GDP fell 13 per cent in 1998 according to IMF figures. The crisis had by this time moved to the much larger and richer economy of South Korea.

The roots of the South Korean crisis lay in weaknesses in the banking system. South Korean banks had absorbed huge amounts of short-term foreign capital after restrictions on foreign borrowing were lifted in 1993. Total short-term external debt increased from US$40 billion in 1993 to $98 billion in September 1997.[8] In June 1997, on the eve of the crisis, short-term debt to foreign banks was twice the level of South Korea's foreign exchange reserves and Korean banks' foreign liabilities amounted to 9.5 per cent of GDP. During the 1990s the government had encouraged Korean banks to lend to the Korean industrial conglomerates known as Chaebol, creating bank assets in Korean won and liabilities in US dollar and thus exposing the banking system to exchange rate risk. By 1996 the Chaebol were heavily indebted to the banks but their underlying competitiveness was beginning to falter. The quality of these loans appeared sound so long as they could be renewed and rolled over when they came due, but in the first half of 1997 the weaknesses in South Korea's inter-linked corporate structure began to be felt. After a fall in steel prices, in January 1997 Hanbo Steel went into bankruptcy, followed by Kia Motors, Korea's third-largest car manufacturer. From July 1997, when liquidity was sucked out of the region by the Thai crisis, Korean bank assets proved to be worthless once the genuine prospects of repayment were revealed. The result was a banking and financial crisis along with the exchange rate crisis. Foreign exchange reserves were run down from US$22.5 billion in October to $6 billion by early December to try to support the exchange rate, but could not forestall a 20 per cent fall against the US dollar. On 4 December 1997, South Korea successfully concluded a rescue package of US$57 billion from the IMF and other multilateral lenders, which was then the largest in history, and the exchange rate of the won was allowed to float. Between July and December 1997, the won lost half of its value against the US dollar with disastrous consequences for the banking system (with its currency mismatch between assets and liabilities) and for Korean industry dependent on imported inputs. The growth in the volume of GDP reversed from 5 per cent in 1997 to –7 per cent in 1998 according to the IMF.

Although these three economies were hardest hit, the East Asian financial crisis had reverberations elsewhere. Malaysia confronted the outflow of capital by controversially imposing exchange controls to prevent capital flight in September 1998. The US dollar value of the Malaysian ringgit fell 50 per cent by the end of 1997 and GDP volume fell 7 per cent in 1998, but Malaysia avoided recourse to the IMF for support with its unwelcome policy conditions. The devaluation of the Taiwan dollar by 10 per cent on 17 October 1997, despite strong economic fundamentals and substantial exchange reserves, renewed speculative pressure in the region, which spread to Hong Kong, newly transferred from British to Chinese sovereignty in July 1997. Taiwan relied less on foreign capital and had embarked on a more gradual process of financial liberalisation, so the economy was more resilient, although it still suffered a drop in exports, slowing growth and rising unemployment. The monetary authorities in Hong Kong, by contrast successfully defended their exchange rate, partly through unorthodox intervention through the stock market to punish speculators, but the property market and stock market crash that ensued had longer-term effects on the Hong Kong economy, and pushed it into unprecedented recession and unemployment. Just as recovery began, the severe acute respiratory syndrome (SARS) health panic of 2002 erupted in Hong Kong with an outbreak of what appeared to be the start of a global pandemic of fatal respiratory infection. This further hurt tourism and business in Hong Kong, and the government turned to the booming mainland economy as the best chance to restore growth. The next year, the Hong Kong SAR government signed the Closer Economic Partnership Agreement (CEPA) to get preferred access to mainland markets for goods and services, and later the services sector benefited from the relaxation of restrictions on tourism for Chinese mainland residents. The PRC had remained insulated from speculation by the inconvertibility of the yuan and controls on financial flows, but it still suffered from weak financial institutions and lack of competitiveness in some sectors. The crisis highlighted the importance of sound governance structures for banks and companies, of transparency about international borrowing and government debt and of careful supervision of banking and financial systems.

A year later, overly optimistic financial markets were at the core of a financial crisis in the Russian Federation in the summer of 1998. In common with Mexico and East Asia, confidence in the glowing prospects of the Russian economy led to a massive inflow of foreign investment, although underlying institutional structures remained weak. The transition to a market economy in the early 1990s had been painful, and growing income inequality and poverty meant that capitalism remained a contested system. In 1995, Russia anchored its anti-inflation policy by pegging the rouble to the US dollar and pledging to cut government spending. Unlike other cases, the current account was fairly balanced and inflows of capital through sales of government debt contributed to the accumulation of reserves, which seemed to bode well for the potential for lenders to be repaid. Capital flowed into the Moscow Stock Exchange and the Russian government was able to raise substantial capital on international markets. After the Asian Financial Crisis shook confidence in emerging markets and oil prices sank, refinancing and servicing the debt became more expensive. The denomination of this debt in foreign currency (mainly US dollars) made it imperative to hold the exchange rate stable, and this absorbed about half of Russia's seemingly ample foreign exchange reserves from mid-1997 to mid-1998. Political instability under the new Yeltsin government in the spring of 1998 added to the waning credibility of the state's ability to service and repay its debt. In a pre-emptive move, on 20 July the IMF pledged US$11.2 billion in support, although it found it difficult to compel the government to implement the conditions attached. The run on the rouble continued, and on 17 August the Russian government suspended debt service, restricted capital outflow and widened the exchange rate band for the rouble. The resulting loss of 70 per cent of the rouble's value in terms of US dollars was much greater than Asian currencies had suffered and inflation reached almost 90 per cent p.a. However, the Russian economy quickly rebounded as local producers replaced imports (which were now much more expensive in local currency) and oil prices rose, raising the revenue derived from Russia's oil and gas industry. The volume of GDP fell by 5 per cent in 1998, but grew by 5 per cent in 1999 and a further 10 per cent in 2000 according to IMF figures.

The final major event in this series of emerging market crises struck Argentina in 2001. As in the other cases, initial optimism about growth prospects and a stable exchange rate (this time embedded in a currency board) encouraged foreign borrowing. After a sharp downturn from the Tequila Effect in 1995, the Argentine economy rebounded and grew by

8 per cent in real terms in 1997, in stark contrast to the experience in most Asian developing countries in that year. In the case of Argentina, government borrowing lay at the foundations of the crisis; when growth slowed, US dollar denominated debt could not be refinanced and a collapse became inevitable. During the 1990s over 90 per cent of public debt was denominated in foreign currency, and the volume of debt rose from one third of GDP in 1995 to over half by 2000.[9] At the same time, exports were only about 10 per cent of GDP and grew much slower than imports in the 1990s, so the ability to service and renew the debt depended on continued inflows of capital. As the ability to finance public debt at the fixed exchange rate set under the currency board system eroded, so too did the credibility of the exchange rate. When growth slowed from 8 per cent to less than 4 per cent in 1998 as a result of domestic political instability, contagion from the rouble crisis and vulnerability to Brazil's downturn, the strains in the system made renewed borrowing even more difficult. The economy entered depression in 1999 with falling output and falling prices due to collapses in consumption and investment, and unemployment soared to 15 per cent in 2000. In this context the public deficit expanded sharply, but the opportunities for international borrowing had contracted and the government had to turn to the IMF. In January 2001 Argentina negotiated extended arrangements with the IMF for US$14 billion of support and also additional co-ordinated bilateral credit of nearly $26 billion from a range of governments underpinned by a commitment to consolidate the public debt. This scheme failed, partly because finance ministers were unable to convince the public or parliament of the need for painful reforms. In June 2001, as output continued to fall, the government arranged to restructure its debt to reduce debt service obligations, but this did not resolve doubts about the government's solvency. In July capital flight was renewed and a further IMF injection of US$5 billion in September 2001 was not enough to restore confidence. Bank runs in November prompted restrictions on the amount of deposits that could be withdrawn each day, but this provoked violent public riots that forced the president to resign in December. By this time the economy was in freefall with output falling 18 per cent in December (year-on-year), and a moratorium on debt payments was announced on 23 December. A new government was formed in January 2002 and the currency board was finally abandoned. The outcome was financial chaos as inflation peaked at 10 per cent per month in April, real GDP fell by 11 per cent over the year as a whole and unemployment soared to 20 per cent. As in previous crises, the rebound in growth was fairly rapid and the volume of GDP increased 9 per cent in 2003, but the political costs lingered.

The depth of the Argentine collapse in the wake of three previous waves of international crises provoked profound criticism over how the international economy was organised and monitored. Part of the problem appeared to arise from pegged exchange rate regimes that prevented smooth incremental adjustment and encouraged the overvaluation of currencies over time. Exiting from these pegs after a build-up of speculative pressure either through devaluation or coming out of a currency board was very costly and destabilising. In this context, flexible or floating exchange rates gained more credence, and countries were encouraged to target their monetary policies at achieving a moderate inflation rate and to let their exchange rates float. As in the wake of the 1982 debacle, the IMF came under particular criticism as a contributor to the depth of the crises rather than providing a solution. On the one hand, the IMF had promoted the market liberalisation that created financial vulnerability and had championed the overly optimistic expectations of the growth prospects for these economies despite their underlying institutional weaknesses. Once a crisis struck, the Fund imposed policies that restrained growth and welfare spending in relatively poor countries with weak institutional structures. Confidence rarely rebounded immediately after an IMF bailout because of doubts about the ability of political leaders to implement draconian policies. Others argued that the inevitability of IMF and World Bank support allowed governments to postpone politically damaging reforms and convinced international investors that they stood a good chance of being bailed out if a sovereign debtor defaulted. The latter criticism falls into the category of moral hazard, in which market interventions produce perverse incentives for borrowers and lenders that encourage them to take on greater risk. As a result, for most of the 2000s the reputation of the Fund was very low and it sought to adapt its operations and restore its relevance. The monitoring role of the IMF was enhanced to try to provide early warning for imbalances so that they could be nipped in the bud rather than blowing up into full-scale crises. The Fund also instituted new ways for members to get quicker access to credit with fewer onerous and time-consuming conditions attached. As we have seen, the Bank for International Settlements embarked on a reform of its rules to develop standards that might better correspond to the risks associated with emerging market crises arising from the private capital market. All these efforts, however, proved inadequate to forestall the greatest and most widespread international economic crisis in 2007–8, as we shall see in the next chapter.

Conclusions and summary

The 1990s demonstrated the weaknesses in the neo-classical free market ideology that had succeeded Keynesian economics from the 1980s. First, the liberalisation of trade in goods and services continued to generate enormous gains for the growth of the international economy, but there was limited commitment to this process by advanced industrial countries with respect to agriculture. Second, the rapid liberalisation of financial markets exposed weak institutions and poor governance in several economies, which prompted damaging systemic crises. Debate raged over reforming the architecture of the international economy, but no effective progress was made. However, the accession of China to the WTO in 2001 and the seemingly inexorable rise of emerging economies such as India and Brazil seemed to promise a new age of successful globalisation as the new millennium began.

7 Lessons not learned

The 2000s

As the 1990s drew to a close, it seemed that the new millennium could usher in a wiser and more balanced period of economic growth that would be immune from the financial crises of preceding decades. While the crises of the 1990s had been painful for emerging economies, these events offered important lessons. The commitment to continued globalisation and faith in its ultimate benefits was unshaken, but the perils of hasty removal of controls, unbridled international borrowing and weak supervision of financial markets had been clearly exposed. Furthermore, the dot.com bust of 2000 reminded the market to be alert to the dangers of irrational exuberance in asset markets. In this contrite atmosphere, public focus shifted to the strains that might be posed by a period of sustained or accelerating growth as economists, scientists and politicians reflected on how the spread of prosperity might affect the global system. As in the halcyon years of the 1960s, when the environmental movement first coalesced, predictions of ever increasing populations and conspicuous consumption prompted concern over the ecological dangers of global warming, threats to biodiversity and, more fundamentally, the survival of the planet. The promise of sustained economic growth also prompted new research on the complex relationship between wealth and happiness.[1] By the end of the decade, however, it was clear that the economic lessons of previous decades had not been learned and the world was plunged into its worst recession since 1945, recalling the doom-laden days of the 1930s.

Economic and monetary union in Europe

As noted in Chapter 5, the Maastricht Treaty of 1992 committed European states to achieving EMU. The political will among the core EU states to make this a reality (after the false start of the Werner Plan in the 1970s) drove the agenda to its successful conclusion in 1999, with the establishment of the European Central Bank (ECB) and the euro, used at first merely as an electronic numeraire for international payments. Euro notes and coins replaced national currencies for twelve members of the EU on 1 January 2002, with only the UK, Sweden and Denmark refusing to take part. These countries were unwilling to accept this solution to the trilemma because of their governments' desire to retain greater policy sovereignty and the option of adjusting their exchange rate to correct external imbalances. Public opinion in these states was generally against joining, although Denmark's referendum in September 2000 rejected the euro by a margin of only 53 per cent to 47 per cent, and 56 per cent of Swedes voted against the euro in their 2003 referendum. British citizens have not been offered a referendum, although opinion polls suggest they are firmly against joining. The initial progress of the euro seemed to vindicate these decisions.

At first, the value of the euro sank in international markets, and although this increased export competitiveness, the ECB eventually had to intervene to provide support for the exchange rate and relax inflationary pressure from depreciation. At its launch in 1999 the euro was worth US$1.17, but by the time cash currency was introduced at the start of 2002 it had fallen to US$0.90. Figure 7.1 shows that as the US dollar began its prolonged depreciation and eurozone economies expanded, the real effective exchange rate of the euro recovered fairly steadily over the following year. Shifting international competitiveness and confidence in the prospects of the eurozone economies has since caused fluctuations in the exchange rate, most sharply in the global financial crisis in the summer of 2008. A further factor affecting the exchange rate was the inclusion of new states, including Greece in 2001, Slovenia on 1 January 2007, Cyprus and Malta on 1 January 2008 and Slovakia on 1 January 2009. The operation of the ECB is also complicated by enlargement, since the Governing Council (the main decision-making body) includes the governors of each of the sixteen eurozone central banks as well as six ECB Executive Board members, which can complicate the determination of a common monetary policy.

While the ECB set a common monetary policy for the eurozone, each member continued to operate its own fiscal policy. This was vital to the independence of the nation states in the system since decisions on taxation and the direction of government spending are deemed central to the democratic responsibilities of national parliaments to their electorates. The impact of government spending patterns on prices and interest rates, however, meant that divergent fiscal policies could undermine or conflict with the ECB's monetary policy goals. In order to try to reduce the strains that this posed for the system, in 1997 members were committed to a 'stability and growth pact' that required them to aim at balanced budgets or small surpluses in the medium term and tasked the European Council and Commission to

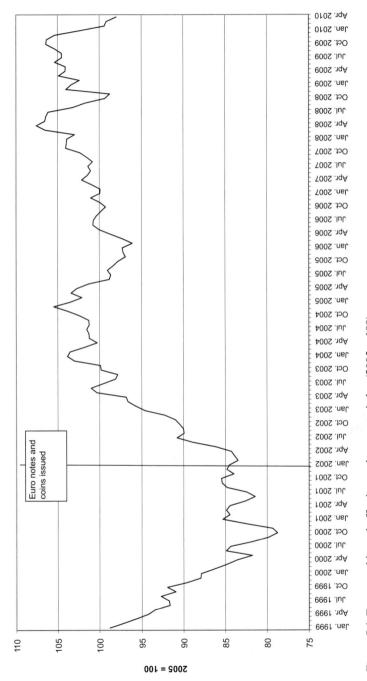

Figure 7.1 Euro monthly real effective exchange rate index (2005 = 100)

Source: Bank for International Settlements

monitor fiscal policy with a view to restraining deficits to less than 3 per cent of GDP and total public debt outstanding to no more than 60 per cent of GDP. In 2004 the European Council found Germany and France in breach of this requirement, but their censure was over-ruled by the European Commission and the terms of the Pact were amended in 2005 to more flexibly take account of particular national economic circumstances in setting appropriate medium-term fiscal targets. Figure 7.2 shows that the 3 per cent limit was not achieved by many members even before the 2008 financial crisis required huge fiscal expenditure. Greece, which as we shall see posed the largest threat to the system, reached a low point in 2004, with a deficit twice the Pact level, and had just begun to approach the 3 per cent limit when the financial crisis struck. Ireland, by contrast, had been in healthy surplus until 2007, but by 2009 had the highest deficit/GDP ratio in the eurozone at over 14 per cent.

In terms of volume of outstanding debt to GDP, Table 7.1 shows that the main outliers were Greece and Italy, which each owed more than their entire GDP output in most years from 1999 to 2009, but the core countries of the system, such as Germany and France, also failed to achieve the Pact targets through the 2000s. Led by the UK, European states adopted fiscal expansion to counteract the depressive effects of the global financial crisis from 2008. During 2009, the euro area countries' deficits as share of GDP rose from 69 per cent to about 79 per cent, although this was unevenly distributed, with the newer members having a lower deficit burden. As we shall see below, the Greek government's consistently high levels of both annual deficit and size of existing borrowing made lenders wary of extending further loans in 2008 and 2009.

In May 2004 the EU embarked on a new era with the accession of ten more states, mainly from Eastern Europe. Post-war European integration was originally aimed at developing a functional economic system, both to avoid future strategic conflict and to cement the recovery of its member states in a democratic capitalist system. It was thus very clearly embedded in the context of the Cold War division of Europe and later the extension of democracy to Greece, Portugal and Spain. The accession process of the 2000s responded to the changing political landscape in Europe once the Cold War had ended and aimed at ensuring the best prospects for economic and social reform across the region. The unwinding of the political borders established after the Second World War offered new opportunities to extend the political and economic institutions of Western Europe. Cyprus, the Czech Republic, Estonia, Hungary, Latvia, Lithuania, Malta, Poland, Slovakia and Slovenia all joined in 2004, followed by Romania and Bulgaria in January 2007. This ambitious expansion drew together a much more diverse range of economies; from Bulgaria with per capita GDP only one

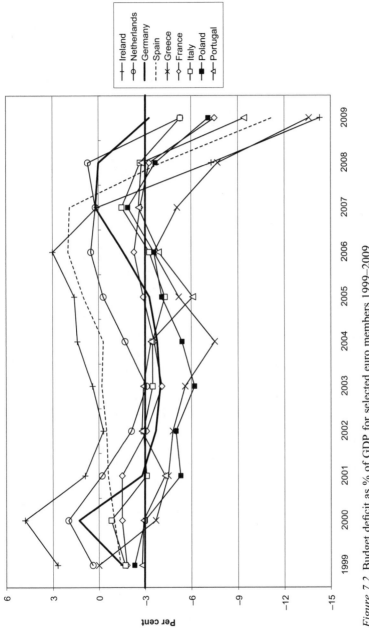

Figure 7.2 Budget deficit as % of GDP for selected euro members 1999–2009

Source: Eurostat

Table 7.1 General government consolidated gross debt as a percentage of GDP

	1999	2000	2001	2002	2003	2004	2005	2006	2007	2008	2009
Italy	113.7	109.2	108.8	105.7	104.4	103.8	105.8	106.5	103.5	106.1	115.8
Greece	94	103.4	103.7	101.7	97.4	98.6	100	97.8	95.7	99.2	115.1
Belgium	113.7	107.9	106.6	103.5	98.5	94.2	92.1	88.1	84.2	89.8	96.7
Euro area (16 countries)	71.7	69.2	68.2	68	69.1	69.5	70.1	68.3	66	69.4	78.7
Hungary	59.8	55	52	55.6	58.4	59.1	61.8	65.6	65.9	72.9	78.3
France	58.9	57.3	56.9	58.8	62.9	64.9	66.4	63.7	63.8	67.5	77.6
Portugal	51.4	50.5	52.9	55.6	56.9	58.3	63.6	64.7	63.6	66.3	76.8
Germany	60.9	59.7	58.8	60.4	63.9	65.8	68	67.6	65	66	73.2
Malta	57.1	55.9	62.1	60.1	69.3	72.3	70.1	63.7	61.9	63.7	69.1
UK	43.7	41	37.7	37.5	39	40.9	42.5	43.5	44.7	52	68.1
Austria	67.2	66.5	67.1	66.5	65.5	64.8	63.9	62.2	59.5	62.6	66.5
Ireland	48.5	37.8	35.6	32.2	31	29.7	27.4	24.9	25	43.9	64
Netherlands	61.1	53.8	50.7	50.5	52	52.4	51.8	47.4	45.5	58.2	60.9
Cyprus	51.8	48.7	52.1	64.6	68.9	70.2	69.1	64.6	58.3	48.4	56.2
Spain	62.3	59.3	55.5	52.5	48.7	46.2	43	39.6	36.2	39.7	53.2
Poland	39.6	36.8	37.6	42.2	47.1	45.7	47.1	47.7	45	47.2	51
Finland	45.7	43.8	42.5	41.5	44.5	44.4	41.7	39.7	35.2	34.2	44
Sweden	64.8	53.6	54.4	52.6	52.3	51.1	50.8	45.7	40.8	38.3	42.3
Denmark	58.1	52.4	49.6	49.5	47.2	45.1	37.8	32.1	27.4	34.2	41.6
Latvia	12.5	12.3	14	13.5	14.6	14.9	12.4	10.7	9	19.5	36.1
Slovenia	:	:	26.8	28	27.5	27.2	27	26.7	23.4	22.6	35.9
Slovakia	47.9	50.3	48.9	43.4	42.4	41.5	34.2	30.5	29.3	27.7	35.7
Czech Republic	16.4	18.5	24.9	28.2	29.8	30.1	29.7	29.4	29	30	35.4
Lithuania	22.8	23.7	23.1	22.3	21.1	19.4	18.4	18	16.9	15.6	29.3
Romania	21.7	22.5	25.7	24.9	21.5	18.7	15.8	12.4	12.6	13.3	23.7
Bulgaria	79.3	74.3	67.3	53.6	45.9	37.9	29.2	22.7	18.2	14.1	14.8

Source: Eurostat

tenth that of Germany, to the small island states of Cyprus and Malta. Figure 7.3 shows the process of convergence of the six poorest EU states toward the EU (27) average per capita income during the years after accession.

The spread of the EU proved highly controversial for existing members, particularly because the extension of the single market allowed the free movement of labour within a much enlarged and economically more diverse territory. Only Denmark, Ireland, Sweden and the UK allowed free movement of labour from new member states immediately upon accession; other countries imposed restrictions for up to seven years, although Finland, Greece, Portugal and Spain abandoned controls after 2006. Because of its relatively open labour market and high incomes, the most popular target for European migrants was the UK, although the proportional impact on Ireland was greater, where the *ex ante* labour force was smaller.[2] Unsurprisingly, the most prominent sending-countries for migrants after 2004 were the relatively low GDP per capita members (Latvia, Lithuania, Poland and Slovakia) and the outflow amounted to between 1 per cent and 2 per cent of their home populations. As well as providing relatively cheap labour in their host countries, these migrants also remitted part of their incomes home. These flows are hard to measure because they are not always reported, but in 2006, about €15 billion was likely sent among EU countries, of which 85 per cent came from EU migrants located in the UK, Germany, Italy and France.[3] Among the new member states the largest recipients were Romania and Poland, which together accounted for almost 40 per cent of the total intra-EU inflows.

A further major challenge prompted by enlargement was the need to reform the CAP, which had become a hugely expensive and unwieldy institution among the fifteen members and promised to be insupportable with the inclusion of ten or twelve more economies with substantial agricultural sectors. The debate in advance of enlargement focused on the conflict between Germany, which wanted to reduce the European price levels and the budget of the CAP, and France, which was the largest beneficiary and resisted eroding the benefits to its farmers. By 1990, the CAP absorbed about 60 per cent of the EU budget and cost European consumers billions more through expensive food costs. Some reforms were introduced to reduce intervention prices and surplus production in 1992, but there was an urgent need for more drastic changes given the imminent participation of millions more farmers. In July 2002 the European Commission proposed cutting the link between production and financial support, shifting the emphasis of CAP toward improving food quality, environmental protection and rural development, as well as reducing the intervention price for some products. In an effort to reduce over-supply, the new scheme meant that farmers would no longer receive higher payments for more production and

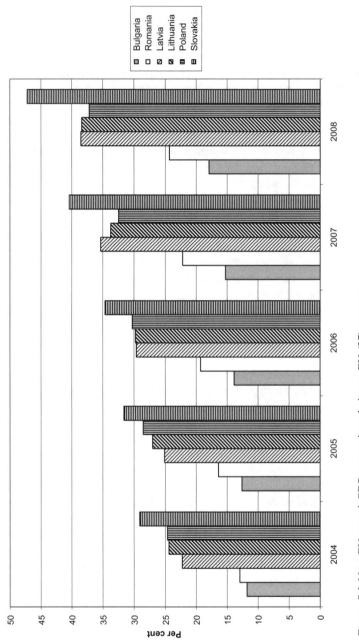

Figure 7.3 New EU states' GDP per capita relative to EU (27) average

Source: Eurostat

instead there would be a single income payment per farm based on payments in 2000–2. In the wake of a series of food scares in the 1980s and 1990s, there was a public need for farms to meet environmental, animal welfare and food safety standards in order to qualify for payments. These proposals were finally accepted in the Luxembourg Agreement of June 2003. The overall size of the CAP budget was fixed at the 2006 level so that when CAP was extended to twenty-seven instead of fifteen countries, the budget was much smaller on a per capita basis. New member states could only access direct payments on a graduated basis, becoming full participants by 2013. By the end of the decade, the CAP absorbed about 40 per cent of the EU budget, a considerable reduction from previous levels.

The dramatic increase in Eastern European migrants to more wealthy Western European economies and reform of the agricultural institutions of the EU were prominent features of the 2000s, but the impact of enlargement on the direction of trade was more muted. There was a significant increase in intra-EU trade for new members states on average in 2004, but for some new entrants such as Poland, Slovenia, Bulgaria and Slovakia, the share of trade with the EU (27) actually fell from 2004–9 and only Romania and Estonia showed a substantial increase in trade with their new partners. Figure 7.4 shows the drop in the intensity of overall intra-EU trade after a rise in the early 2000s. This pattern signals the increasingly global nature of international trade and rising commodity prices that together contributed to rising shares for non-EU trading partners, in particular China and oil producing states. Predictably, the country with the least trade integration with the enlarged EU was the UK, the so-called reluctant partner, where only 53 per cent of imports came from other EU states in 2008 and 2009. This relatively detached trade pattern was consistent with Britain's distinctive historical relationship with the process of European integration, starting from the initial refusal to take part in Messina in 1955, slow accession to the ERM in the 1980s and retaining its own national currency instead of adopting the euro in 1999.

As well as economic changes, enlargement also fundamentally altered the political nature of the EU since the administrative institutions that had been struggling to cope with fifteen members became even more unwieldy for twenty-seven. This prompted a new and controversial phase of reform to broaden and strengthen the EU constitution and balance the democratic rights of the few large richer states as against the greater number of smaller members. After years of drafting, the Treaty establishing a Constitution for Europe was signed on 29 October 2004 but was rejected by referenda in France and the Netherlands in May and June 2005. This provoked a new round of compromise, culminating in the Treaty of Lisbon, which amended the core terms of the EU rather than proposing a more ambitious

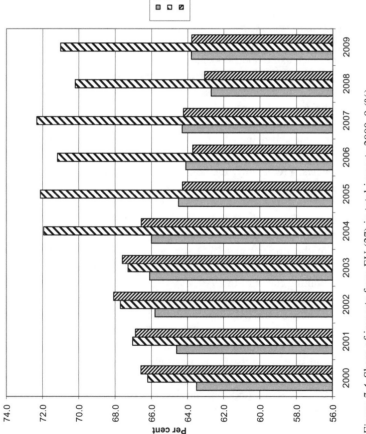

Figure 7.4 Share of imports from EU (27) in total imports 2000–9 (%)

Source: Eurostat

'Constitution'. It was signed by EU Heads of State in December 2007 and sent for ratification by the member states. The terms of the new Treaty provoked hostility: small states wanted to protect the powers of the European Commission and feared being marginalised by a strengthened European Council; large states wanted to protect their leadership position as the largest contributors to the budget; and many states wanted to retain a veto on policies such as immigration, social policy or human rights. Politicians learned from the debacle of the Constitution about the dangers of applying directly to popular vote, and Ireland was the only state to hold a public referendum on the Treaty. In June 2008 the Irish rejected the Treaty with 53 per cent opposed, but a second vote in 2009 gained 67 per cent approval. After some amendments, the Treaty was finally ratified by the parliaments of all states by the end of 2009, ushering in new voting patterns in the European Council of Ministers, more powers for the European Parliament, a new post of European Minister for Foreign Affairs and a more permanent European Council President rather than a half-yearly revolving seat for each member.

The distinction between creating institutions to promote economic integration and merging national political or strategic priorities had always been controversial, as was evident even before the EEC was founded in the rejection of the European Defence Community in 1954. After the creation of the eurozone in 1999, the ability to pursue independent fiscal policies (with the attendant impact on social expenditure) eroded, but the desire to pursue national priorities did not abate. The inability to resolve this tension in the trilemma between national policy sovereignty and fixed exchange rates in a context of open capital markets resulted in a compromise in 1999 that established a ECB, which operated and issued a common currency for members, but did not have a coherent economic policy context in which monetary policy was formulated. Convergence criteria were set to establish 'rules' for members in terms of inflation rates and budget deficits, but they were not easily enforced and were breached by core members, such as France. Through the first decade of the eurozone's operation, the contradiction was hidden by generally healthy growth rates, moderate inflation and a strong euro. The global financial crisis of 2008, however, soon exposed the flaws in the system in a way that proved extremely costly to both the eurozone members and the international community through the IMF.

While the enlargement of 2004 and 2007 fundamentally changed the nature of the EU and seemed to pose huge challenges to achieve convergence, by the end of the decade it was the members of the second enlargement in the 1980s that posed a direct threat to the integrity of the system. The Greek economy was particularly exposed, with large government deficits and a current account deficit of 11 per cent of GDP in 2006 (second only to Iceland in the OECD) rising to 14.5 per cent in 2008 according to OECD figures. The Greek fiscal deficit as a proportion of GDP rose from 4 per cent in 2006 to 14 per cent by 2009, and total public debt outstanding was 115 per cent of GDP. The competitiveness of Greek exports had receded but since Greece was in the eurozone, depreciation was not a possible solution to correct the external imbalance. Unit labour costs in Greece, which are a measure of labour productivity, were about the same as the euro area average in 2006 but rose to 110 per cent by the end of 2009 (OECD figures, based on a 2005 = 100 index). International investors began to anticipate a default on existing debt, and this made it impossible for Greece to refinance or roll over its obligations. At the end of April 2010 the gap in the yield on Greek ten-year bonds compared to a benchmark German bond exceeded 8 per cent p.a. It seemed that the future of the eurozone itself was in peril as some commentators suggested that Greece would have to pull out of the euro to devalue. On 9 May, euro-area members agreed to a €80 million bailout in conjunction with a €30 billion stand-by credit from the IMF (SDR26.4 billion). The IMF loan was equivalent to thirty-two times the Greek quota in the IMF, the largest ever credit in these terms. In comparison, the 1997 South Korean bailout was 'merely' sixteen times the South Korean quota. In absolute terms the value was less than previous credits offered to Brazil (2003, SDR27.4 billion) and Mexico (2009, SDR31.5 billion), but, unlike the case of Greece, these credits were mainly precautionary and not intended to be drawn. In return for this package of support, the Greek government had to adopt a drastic austerity programme including civil service pay and pension cuts, higher taxes, general wage freezes and raising the retirement age. The eurozone also agreed to establish the European Financial Stability Facility to provide up to €440 billion in loans to members in financial difficulty, loans that were guaranteed by the member states of the eurozone. Other countries that joined the European Community in the 1980s, such as Portugal and Spain, also imposed strict fiscal policies to ward off changes in market sentiment that would make it more difficult for them to borrow. In November 2010 a second bail-out was negotiated for Ireland totalling €67.5 billion in external support from the IMF (€22.5 billion) and the EU (€45 billion). The sixty-year-old European project of economic integration without political union appeared to have survived these major attacks, but clearly some further reform was necessary.

The BRIC phenomenon

China's dramatic success at penetrating international markets generated optimism that market-orientated reforms in other countries could lead to similar outcomes elsewhere. During the 2000s many commentators claimed to be witnessing a fundamental shift in the global economy toward a collection dubbed the BRICs by Goldman Sachs in 2001: Brazil, Russia, India and China.[4] These countries combined large populations with complementary economic structures: commodities in Russia and Brazil, services in India, and manufacturing in China. Together they promised to be the next set of fast-growing emerging markets. Figure 7.5 shows that, although Brazil's performance was well below the developing country average, the others were all well above. The clear leader was the Chinese economy. Figure 7.6 shows the rising share of these countries in world trade from 2001, but it is clear that the largest contribution was China's extraordinary economic performance.

These countries shared rather little in common other than market-orientated, outward-looking reforms and predictions of sustainable rapid economic growth. The experience of China in achieving highly competitive manufacturing based on labour-intensive production by foreign-invested companies has already been discussed. The Russian economy was driven by oil and gas exploitation and the rising price of crude oil during the 2000s, but the domestic economic system became increasingly concentrated in the hands of a few so-called 'oligarchs' and the political regime under President Putin was increasingly authoritarian. The Indian economy thrived on its human capital, cheap labour and innovations in communications, which made it a major player in the global redistribution of the services trade during this decade. Call centres, medical imaging and a huge selection of other services that could be traded through the internet bloomed in the teeming urban centres of Mumbai and Delhi. Still, poor infrastructure meant that traffic gridlock and periodic power shortages constrained development potential. Brazil's economic success owed much to commodity price booms in agricultural products such as soy, as well as from surging demand for minerals and raw materials such as aluminium and bauxite, partly due to the rapid industrial expansion of China.

Despite their differences, these states seemed poised at the end of the decade to become a more important feature of the world economic system, holding their first quadripartite summit in Russia in June 2009, where they called for changes in the governance of the international economy to be more inclusive. At the end of the decade, they appeared to have weathered the global economic crisis fairly well; Russia and Brazil were particularly hard hit, but Brazil was one of the first emerging market countries to recover strongly. India's banking system proved robust to the international financial crisis and growth slowed but did not reverse, while China suffered a trade shock but also recovered swiftly.

Figure 7.5 BRICs real GDP growth rates 2000–7

Source: UNCTAD

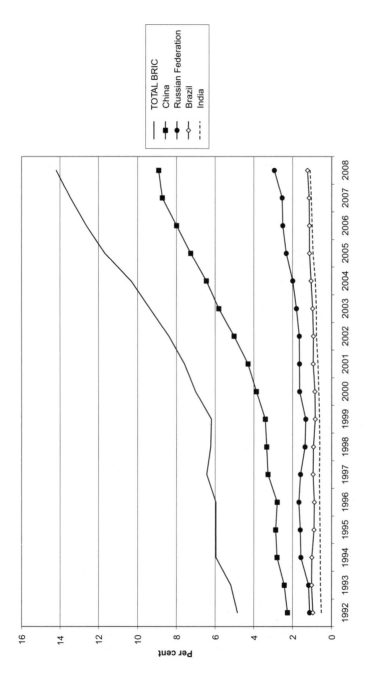

Figure 7.6 BRIC countries: Share of world trade 1992–2008 (%)

Source: UNCTAD

Global imbalance

The key development in the international economy during the 2000s was the growing imbalance among persistent surplus and deficit countries led by the accumulation of enormous current account deficits by the United States. The gap between American spending on imported goods and the proceeds of exports ballooned from US$430 billion in 2001 to $830 billion by 2007.[5] Figure 7.7 shows nominal current account balances for a range of countries that ran persistent surpluses in the run-up to the 2007 global financial crisis. Rising oil prices after 2001 contributed to trade surpluses for Russia and other oil producing states in the Middle East. Weak domestic demand in the Japanese economy generated substantial trade surpluses, but the largest single contributor to the global imbalance on the surplus side was China. Over the five years from 2001, China gradually liberalised its markets in accordance with the terms of its accession to the WTO, but as discussed in Chapter 6, cheap labour, inflows of capital and the pegged exchange rate meant that trade surpluses continued to mount.

The US external deficit was reflected in rising internal government deficits as domestic spending was financed by borrowing abroad. The American government under George W. Bush embarked on two expensive overseas conflicts in Iraq and Afghanistan after the terrorist attack on New York in September 2001, but the Republican administration was also committed to relatively low tax rates so the government was required to increase its borrowing. Under Ronald Reagan's administration in the 1980s net government debt rose from the equivalent of one quarter of the nation's GDP in 1980 to a peak of 55 per cent in 1994. The Clinton administration then shrank the ratio to a low of 34 per cent by 2001, but George W. Bush ratcheted up borrowing, so that net government debt was over 40 per cent of GDP in each year from 2002–7 (according to IMF figures). This internal debt position of the world's largest economy had important global implications.

Countries running persistent surpluses need to store them in the form of reserves, and since the US dollar is the primary international currency, most countries in surplus bought up US Treasury bills and other US government debt for this purpose. In 2001 foreign governments and other official entities bought US$55 billion worth of US government securities, but by 2006 this flow amounted to $428 billion, most of which was in the form of short-term US Treasury bills, according to the Bureau of Economic Affairs (BEA). The enhanced demand for US government assets to hold as foreign exchange reserves helped to finance American debt at low rates of interest, keeping wholesale and retail interest rates lower than they otherwise would be. In this sense, the international role of the US dollar meant that the global

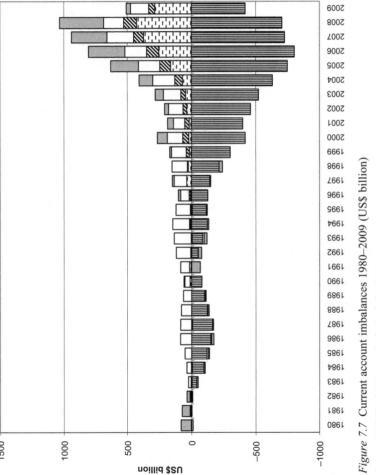

Figure 7.7 Current account imbalances 1980–2009 (US$ billion)

Source: IMF World Economic Outlook Database

imbalance fuelled the domestic US debt boom underpinning the greatest financial crisis of the post-war period.

This cause of the 2007–8 financial crisis can be traced back to the organisation of the international monetary system in the 1940s, when Keynes' proposal for a neutral international reserve asset not connected with a national economy was rejected in favour of a US-dollar standard. Under Bretton Woods, countries that pegged to the US dollar tended to retain US dollars as reserve assets in order to protect their exchange rate. From the 1970s, many countries abandoned a bilateral currency peg, but the US dollar continued as the main reserve asset. Most commodities including oil were denominated in US dollar, so there were commercial reasons for some countries to retain working balances in US dollars. Furthermore, the large and liquid market in US-denominated assets made American government securities an attractive method of storing value. The combined attractions of liquidity and the widespread use and acceptability of the US dollar for commercial transactions, meant that the dollar retained its role as the main global currency, despite the fall in its exchange rate after 2002. During the 2000s there was some shift toward other reserve assets, partly due to the fall in the value of the dollar, but about two thirds of recorded global reserves were still held as US dollars during the 2000s. About one quarter of global reserve assets were held in euro by 2005, but European markets were not as liquid as those for US dollar assets and recent problems for the euro suggest its share may not increase soon.[6] The yen was another option, but the Japanese economy was not strong and interest rates approaching 0 per cent discouraged the use of the yen as a reserve currency, so it comprised only about 4 per cent of global reserves in the 2000s. The Chinese yuan was not easily convertible and there was no market for Chinese government debt available to foreigners, so it could not be used as a reserve asset.

Because the dollar's international role appeared to contribute to the persistence of the global imbalance and fuelled the expansion of credit in the United States, one of the reactions to the global financial crisis was calls to replace the dollar with some other asset that could be more deliberately managed to protect the stability of the international monetary system. Thus, in March 2009, Zhou Xiaochuan of the People's Bank of China supported calls from Joseph Stiglitz and others to develop the SDR into a genuine reserve asset.[7] Chapter 3 showed how the problem of using a national currency as an international reserve asset had prompted the origins of the SDR in the late 1960s, but it never operated as originally intended. With no secondary market or commercial use, the SDR was not an attractive store of value or means of exchange; two of the defining characteristics of money. It was used as a unit of account by the IMF and sometimes as a short-cut to define a basket currency peg (since its value was based on a range of prominent national currencies), but its development was stunted during the 1970s and 1980s by the resurgence of the US dollar due to the oil crises and the dominance of the American economy. By 2008, SDRs amounted to less than half of 1 per cent of global reserves so resurrecting it as a replacement for existing foreign exchange reserves or even promoting future accumulations to erode the role of national currencies in reserves in the future was a heroic suggestion. In 2009, as part of efforts to expand global liquidity, the IMF distributed a further US$287 billion worth of SDR, but this only brought the total SDR issued to 3.75 per cent of global reserves (including gold). With huge obstacles in the way of creating a system to make the global imbalance more sustainable, attention was primarily focused on reducing the imbalance itself.

Since trade liberalisation from the mid-1990s did not lead to the rebalancing of China's trade accounts, the United States, the IMF and other developed nations increased pressure on China to appreciate its currency in order to reduce the price competitiveness of its production in world markets. By the 2000s China was one of the few major economies with an exchange rate pegged to the US dollar, and it was still using the exchange rate set in 1994. For several years China resisted these calls on the basis that the Chinese yuan was not fundamentally undervalued, that China's financial institutions were too fragile to cope with a more flexible exchange rate and that it was labour competitiveness rather than the exchange rate that was determining the success of China's exports. As the 2000s progressed, however, these arguments became more difficult to sustain since the US dollar underwent a prolonged depreciation on global markets taking the Chinese yuan with it. Figure 7.8 shows how the price of the US dollar compared with its main trading partners fell fairly steadily from a peak at the beginning of 2002 until the depths of the global financial crisis in July 2008. The crisis prompted a rush back to US dollars by global investors seeking some security and the exchange rate appreciated thereafter. The effective exchange rate of the Chinese yuan closely followed the US dollar during the period in which the exchange rates were pegged to each other so that the yuan got steadily cheaper on world markets while China's balance-of-payments surplus surged. The result was that China's foreign exchange reserves grew from US$212 billion in 2001 to US$819 billion by 2005, most of which was loaned to the US government through the purchase of Treasury bills and other US government debt.

In July 2005 the Chinese authorities finally ended the peg to the US dollar and began to appreciate the yuan gradually within a more flexible system whereby the value of the yuan was determined against the currencies of a range of its trading partners. At first, this resulted in only a small appreciation against the US dollar, but by 2008 the yuan had risen in value by about

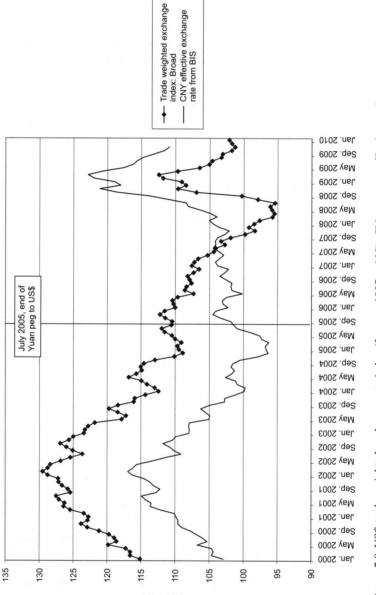

Figure 7.8 US$ trade-weighted exchange rate index (January 1997 = 100); Chinese yuan effective exchange rate

Source: Board of Governors of the Federal Reserve System, http://research.stlouisfed.org/fred2/series/TWEXBMTH/downloaddata?cid=105

20 per cent against the US dollar. Unfortunately, this appreciation did not have the anticipated effects on the Chinese balance of trade. Far from reducing the surplus, fresh inward flows of investment and an ever increasing trade surplus drove China's foreign exchange reserves to over US$1.5 trillion by 2007. In the midst of the crisis in July 2008 as China's trade dropped, the yuan was re-pegged to the US dollar to provide an element of stability.

As well as the systemic imbalance, there were other shocks to the international economy in the late 2000s that contributed to the fragile environment. After a decade of nominal stability in the price of crude oil at around US$20 per barrel, Figure 7.9 shows that the price began to rise sharply in 2003 as a result of conflict in the Middle East and OPEC controls on production. The price peaked at an average value of US$132 per barrel in July 2008 causing costs of industrial production and transport to rise sharply on the eve of the financial crisis. Food prices also spiked in 2008 (partly due to a shortage of rice) reducing disposable incomes in developing countries and destabilising commodity markets further.

While the global imbalance, high levels of domestic debt and commodity price shocks were facilitating factors for the global financial crisis of 2007–8, the main systemic weakness was the fragility of national and international financial markets. In particular, the mismanagement of risk meant that banks and other financial institutions were left vulnerable to a contagious loss of confidence that stripped their balance sheets of apparently valuable assets, leaving them at best illiquid and at worst insolvent. The unprecedented size and global integration of financial markets spread the impact of these failures around the world. From 1999 to 2008 the value of banks' foreign assets soared from about 300 times global GDP to 500 times (according to BIS figures). Figure 7.10 shows the dramatic rise in the value of debt securities outstanding and that most of this rise in activity was due to issues by financial institutions rather than corporations that produced other goods and services, or governments.

Table 7.2 gives an indication of the pace of growth of a range of international financial products both in nominal terms and compared to estimates of the size of global production. The most striking expansion was in the value of international debt securities and international bonds and notes, categories that both rose to be equivalent to almost half of world GDP from less than 10 per cent in 1990. By far the largest category, however, was over-the-counter derivatives. These were opaque instruments that can be difficult to understand. Some can be interpreted as bets on the movements of other markets (so their value is 'derived' from the foreign exchange market, commodities market or equity market) and some were bets on whether credits would be defaulted on – so-called credit default swaps,

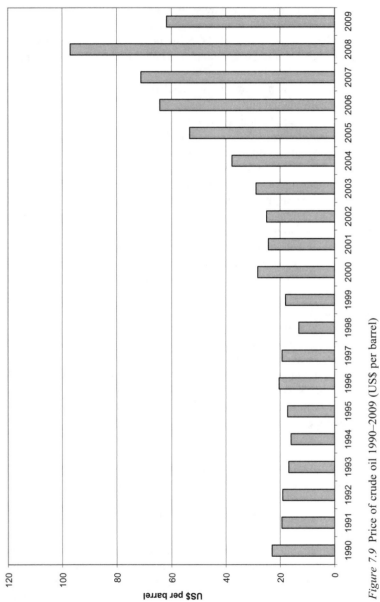

Figure 7.9 Price of crude oil 1990–2009 (US$ per barrel)

Source: IMF, *International Financial Statistics*

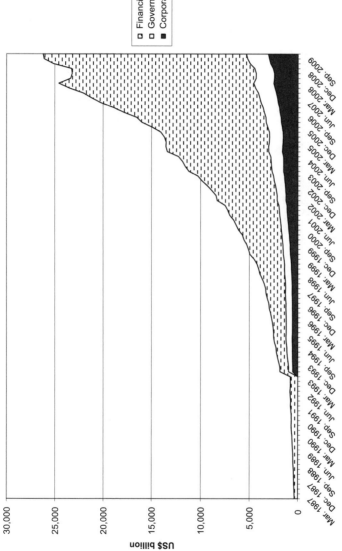

Figure 7.10 International debt securities: Amounts outstanding by issuer (US$ billion) quarterly, March 1987 to December 2009

Source: Bank for International Settlements

Table 7.2 Value of international financial products 1990–2009 (US$ billion)

	1990	1995	2000	2005	2007	2009
Nominal value						
International debt securities	1644.67	2848.24	6490.34	14,602.32	22,705.06	27,010.26
International bonds and notes	1555.35	2696.68	5996.52	13,951.87	21,568.31	26,078.18
International money market instruments	89.32	151.56	493.82	650.45	1136.75	932.09
International equity issues (announced)	3.78	22.38	54.05	105.87	164.53	247.64
OTC derivatives		72,134.26*	95,199.50	299,260.85	595,738.43	614,673.60
World GDP	22,823.02	29,620.65	31,941.92	45,090.30	54,840.87	54,863.55
As a percent of world GDP						
International debt securities	7.21	9.62	20.32	32.38	41.40	49.23
International bonds and notes	6.81	9.10	18.77	30.94	39.33	47.53
International money market instruments	0.39	0.51	1.55	1.44	2.07	1.70
International equity issues	0.02	0.08	0.17	0.23	0.30	0.45
OTC derivatives		225.83*	298.04	663.69	1086.30	1120.37

Source: BIS Banking Data. *June 1998 figure.

which financial institutions used to hedge their risk exposure. 'Over the counter' means that these products are not traded in an organised exchange but instead form contracts privately agreed between the participating parties. This makes them hard to regulate and supervise and some argued they contributed to the contagion in the financial crisis of 2008 when some players found themselves over-exposed to large adverse market movements.

During the 2000s, innovation in the range of products that securitised existing debt eroded the transparency of banks' operations; it appears in hindsight that even the board members of some institutions had only a hazy understanding of some of these products. With rising liquidity and increased lending against property, banks sought to repackage their loans into newly collected assets and sell them on to other institutions. The direct link between lender and borrower was thus broken as lenders were able to sell on their risky loans in complex packages that mixed them up with more robust assets. As they became more complex, the value of these packages, known as securitised lending, became more difficult to judge. The Basel II rules suggested that residential property mortgages could be considered as the equivalent of between AAA and A+ corporate or sovereign claims, but this turned out to be a dramatic over-estimation of their quality.[8] In the liquid American market, new sectors of the population were brought into mortgage borrowing sometimes at very high ratio of loans to value (well over 100 per cent) and with little evidence of credit-worthiness required by the borrower. These so-called sub-prime loans generated high nominal returns since higher interest rates were charged for these loans than for more credit-worthy borrowers, but at considerably greater risk of default. Through securitisation, lenders believed that they had transferred this risk to other financial institutions, but in fact their exposure to systemic fragility was increased. When the US property market turned downward, borrowers that could not keep up their payments were no longer able to pay off their mortgage by selling the house and they defaulted, wiping out the assets from the balance sheets of banks and other financial institutions. Because this form of lending had permeated the market through securitisation, the impact led to a contraction of credit that soon spread throughout the global financial system. As concerns about the underlying quality of bank assets grew, it became more difficult for banks to access the global money market. From July 2006 to July 2007 the London inter-bank lending rate for sterling (three-month LIBOR) rose steadily from less than 5 per cent to just over 6 per cent.

As global money markets contracted, those institutions that depended on them were squeezed. In the UK, Northern Rock was a regional mortgage lender that had borrowed substantial funds in money markets to lend on to its customers; up to 70 per cent of its funds came from the wholesale money market rather than the traditional route of attracting funds from depositors. In effect, Northern Rock borrowed short term and loaned the funds out on long-term mortgages at attractive interest rates for up to 125 per cent of the value of properties. Its operations depended on a constant flow of cash and when this dried up, rumours that the bank would not be able to meet its liabilities encouraged hundreds of depositors to queue up to withdraw their funds in September 2007. Although these retail deposits were guaranteed by the UK government, the threat of a bank run prompted the Prime Minister to announce publicly on 13 September that the government would meet all of Northern Rock's liabilities and effectively nationalised the bank. This set a precedent for the British government strategy of bailing out failing banks, which would be applied a year later to Royal Bank of Scotland, Lloyds TSB and HBOS. Meanwhile, the US Treasury took a different approach and allowed the traumatic collapse of Lehman Brothers investment house when it was similarly hit by a solvency crisis due to the contraction of credit markets and losses on mortgage backed assets.

Lehman Brothers had been actively involved in trading the securitised mortgage debt associated with the expansion of sub-prime lending during the 2000s and was forced to write off substantial amounts of its assets during the first half of 2008. After announcing huge losses in September 2008 its share price plummeted, but unlike Northern Rock the US government refused to be a lender of last resort. The 158-year-old company was forced to close on 15 September 2008, marking the biggest bankruptcy in US history. The Lehman collapse caused a rash of panic across the globe as it defaulted on its international liabilities, and this drained further liquidity out of financial markets as creditors everywhere sought to cash in their assets. Two other global players, Morgan Stanley and AIG, were left on the brink of bankruptcy and it seemed the entire international financial system was about to implode. Stock markets around the world collapsed, wiping out trillions of dollars of value from global companies. In the face of imminent disaster and recriminations over its handling of Lehman, the US government agreed to bail out AIG to try to stabilise the situation, but markets continued to stumble. On 29 September the US Congress rejected the Treasury's plan to buy up the devalued assets from bank balance sheets in order to restore their liquidity, and global markets shuddered a step closer to collapse. Congress agreed a revised plan a few days later on 3 October to provide up to US$700 billion of support for the banking system, but the cascading erosion of confidence postponed the restoration of orderly market operations.

Around the world, governments bailed out their banking systems, took equity ownership of some banks, lowered interest rates and provided extra liquidity to try to get the financial markets to function normally again.

Despite their excesses in the 2000s, and public castigation of reckless behaviour, national banking systems had to be restored to provide credit to industry, services and international trade in order to sustain real economic activity even at a high cost for taxpayers. The most desperate case was the small economy of Iceland (population c. 319,000 in 2008), which had become completely dominated by international financial services based in three large global banks: Glitner, Landsbanki and Kaupthing. Table 7.3 shows that the banking sector accounted for 0.04 per cent of firms but 61 per cent of total assets of enterprises in Iceland in 2007. Moreover, equity fell from 15 per cent of total assets of banks to 12 per cent from 2006 to 2007 compared with other enterprises where equity was 39 per cent of total assets in 2006 and 37 per cent in 2007.

As the global money market contracted during September and October 2008, the ability of Iceland's banks to finance the aggressive international expansion of their balance sheets evaporated. They were so large compared to the Icelandic economy, that a complete bailout was impossible; their liabilities were reported to be six times Iceland's GDP. The bankruptcy wiped out deposits of investors around the world, even prompting the UK to employ terrorism legislation to freeze these banks' assets in the UK. The Icelandic currency, the kroner, fell sharply on international markets, adding to inflation that reached a peak of 17 per cent p.a. in November 2008, and the IMF agreed a loan package of US$2.1 billion to try to stabilise the economy. In 2009 the population of Iceland fell for the first time since 1889 as almost 5,000 Icelandic citizens moved to find opportunities elsewhere, 30 per cent going to Denmark and 30 per cent to Norway.[9] In a sense, Iceland was a microcosm of the financial excesses of the 2000s, with rapid extension into risky markets by a few organisations that exposed the public to huge burdens of unemployment and financial loss.

On a global scale, international trade collapsed and unemployment soared during 2008, seeming to threaten another Great Depression to rival that of

Table 7.3 Statistics of enterprises in Iceland

Sector	Number of enterprises		Total assets (= total liabilities + total equity)		Total equity	
	2006	2007	2006	2007	2006	2007
Total	31,047	28,370	12.75	16.94	3.2	3.74
Financial intermediation	114	105	7.58	10.4	1.18	1.27
Other	30,933	28,265	5.17	6.54	2.02	2.47

Source: Statistics Iceland ('Financial intermediation' excludes insurance and pension funding)

the 1930s. However, signs of recovery began in the spring of 2009 when banks began to report profits and growth began to recover, with particularly strong prospects for China. Having learned the lesson of the 1930s, co-ordinated expansionist policies around the world appeared to have staved off a prolonged collapse, and by 2010 most economies were tentatively crawling out of recession. However, many countries such as the UK were left with huge fiscal deficits that threatened the longer-term recovery.

Figure 7.11 shows the movements in share prices of companies from the United States, Europe, Africa and Asia. African and Asian companies had the most volatile market prices, both falling further and recovering faster than companies operating in more established economies in the United States and Europe. By the end of 2009, US share prices were back close to prices in mid-2006, but European company share values were still only at the levels of early 2005. Europe's woes were compounded by strains in the eurozone monetary system. With corporate share values bouncing back and bank profits recovering, taxpayers were poised to pay the burden of the crisis.

Global recession

Figure 7.12 puts the 2009 global recession into a longer-term perspective, where the impact on growth rates was clearly more severe than the two global downturns associated with the oil crises in the 1970s and 1980s.

Figure 7.13 shows the collapse in international trade associated with the global recession. The contraction in trade affected all countries, most suffering declines of at least 20 per cent, and also covered a wide range of products. The growth of exports from China and developing countries was much faster than advanced economies in the months running up to the crisis, but they then fell faster. Overall, world exports fell by close to a quarter, but this was not distributed evenly. The poorest developing countries were among the hardest hit, particularly in Africa where the value of exports fell by about half. China, the powerhouse of the international trading system, was not immune to this crisis as it had been in 1997. The impact on China's trade was almost immediate, and exports fell from a peak in September 2008 of US$136 billion to a low in February 2009 of $65 billion, although the recovery was equally swift. Other developing countries recovered more slowly than world trade as a whole. Once again, gyrations in the international economy widened the gap between rich and poor states.

Although analysis is still underway, it seems the collapse in international trade was driven by consumer uncertainty that led to postponed purchases and secondarily to the freezing of short- and medium-term credit needed to finance trade. In addition, the fall in commodity prices from their high levels on the eve of the crisis exaggerated the collapse in the value of world trade.

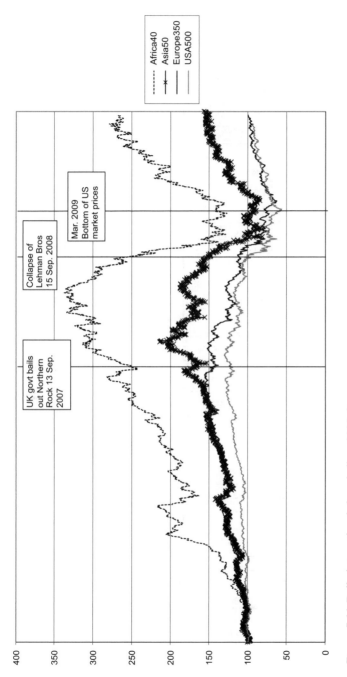

Figure 7.11 Daily international share indices 2005–9

Note: USA500 is a broad index of 500 American companies; Europe350 is a broad index of 350 European companies from 17 countries; Africa40 includes large companies operating exclusively in Africa; Asia50 are companies listed in Hong Kong, Taiwan, Singapore and South Korea.
Source: Standard and Poor

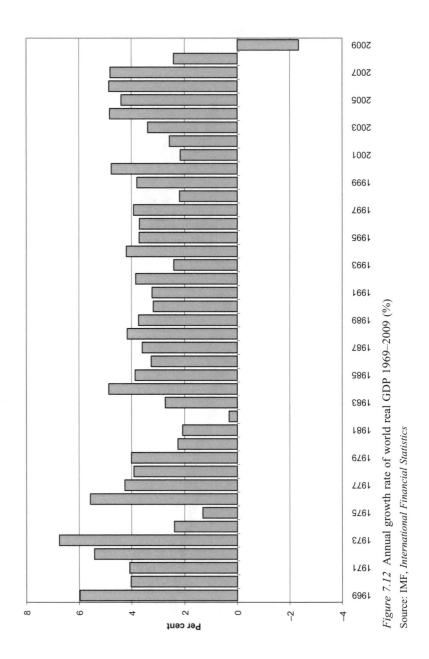

Figure 7.12 Annual growth rate of world real GDP 1969–2009 (%)

Source: IMF, *International Financial Statistics*

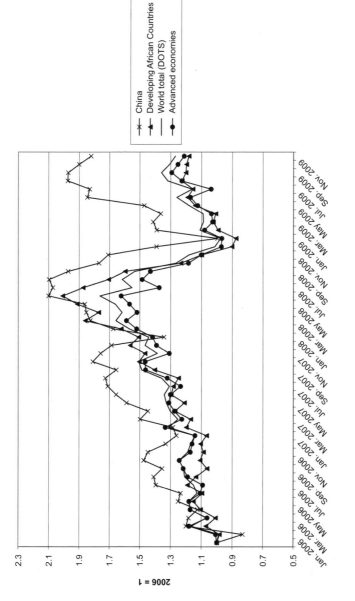

Figure 7.13 Value of global exports 2006–9 (January 2006 = 1)

Source: IMF, *Direction of Trade Statistics*

In historical perspective, the fall in the initial months of the crisis was sharper than during 1929–30 at the beginning of the Great Depression, although trade volumes recovered faster, beginning to turn around after about ten months.[10] The increased integration of production processes around the world and complex global supply chains increased the synchronicity of the downturn so that imports and exports fell simultaneously.

Unlike the financial and currency crises of the 1990s that had their origins in emerging markets, the origins of the global financial crisis appeared to be due to lax regulation and greedy banks in rich countries such as the United States. This threw open the question of the governance of the international economic system. Since the war, the core industrialised countries had set the agenda; first through Anglo-American co-operation at Bretton Woods, then by the United States and Europe leading the process of economic integration in the 1950s and 1960s, and then by the United States and Japan as the world's largest economies. The core institutions that monitored international economic relations were located in and dominated by the United States and Europe – such as the IMF, the World Bank, the BIS and the WTO. The demonstrable failure of these institutions to forestall the worst and most widespread recession of the post-war period provided an opportunity for states that were peripheral to decision-making but central to the global economy. Legitimate proposals to reform the international system could no longer be delivered by a closed G7 forum of wealthy states, which no longer seemed to reflect the reality of economic leadership and in particular excluded the fast-growing and influential BRICs.

The G7 had been formed to deal with market instability in 1976 and included smaller economies such as Italy and Canada, which had been diplomatically important, as well as engaging Japan as a rising economic power. After the 1990s crisis the importance of emerging markets to global economic stability prompted the creation of the G20, which aimed at including a broader range of countries in global economic governance, although a quarter of the seats were still taken by the members of the EU.[11] It was obviously easier to add members to the group than to replace existing countries with new members. During the 2000s, this body was effectively sidelined by the continued domination of the G7, but in April 2008 the G20 was revived at a summit in Washington to address the global financial crisis. Later, at the Pittsburg Summit of 2009 the leaders of the G20 pledged to make this group 'the premier forum for our international economic cooperation'. The IMF and World Bank were also represented at G20 meetings, and this group was used to co-ordinate macro-economic expansion in the midst of the crisis to forestall a depression, and to strengthen international financial institutions such as the IMF. In April 2009, the G20 agreed to strengthen oversight of the global economy through a Financial Stability

Board (FSB), which sought to co-ordinate the supervision and regulation of international financial markets by bringing together national regulators as well as the IMF, BIS, OECD, World Bank and other organisations responsible for promoting financial stability.[12] An important element in the G20 negotiations was the agenda to rebalance governance in the World Bank and the IMF, where voting rights arising from historically based quota contributions privileged the United States and Europe at the expense of the BRICs and other emerging economies. Unlike the crises of the 1990s, the 2008 global financial crisis restored the IMF to the centre of policy-making as it became part of the G20 management, increased its resources and representativeness, and reforming the much-reviled conditionality of its loans. In March 2009 a series of reforms was announced to tailor conditionality, increase the amount and accessibility of funds, and introduce new products such as the emergency Flexible Credit Line for members with strong underlying economic structures in short-term financial stress. This marked a return to the spirit of the original Articles of Agreement as they were designed in the 1940s; to provide short-term credit for short-term balance-of-payments problems and thereby prevent recourse to systemically damaging contractionary policies when their economies were not in 'fundamental disequilibrium'.

We noted in Chapter 2 that the organisation of international economic relations after 1945 was based on the diagnosis of the causes of the Great Depression and the collected determination among the world's leaders to prevent a repeat of the uncoordinated beggar-thy-neighbour policies that contributed to the misery of the 1930s. In the aftermath of the 2008 global crisis, it is tempting to suggest that the world is about to embark on a fresh reform of the international financial architecture that will prevent a repeat of the chaos in financial markets and the shock to growth, trade and employment that ensued. This time, however, the solution to the trilemma is being determined by markets that have grown well beyond the size and control of national governments. Rather than try to restrict international capital flows, the G20 hopes to restore and sustain economic growth through a combination of flexible exchange rates, robust open markets and co-ordinated macro-economic policy. Faith in the efficient functioning of markets without prudential supervision to ensure transparency has been shattered by two decades of worsening financial crises. As in the wake of every financial crisis since the Second World War, the current crisis has prompted efforts at greater co-ordination of financial regulation. Whether governments' desire for national sovereignty over banking and monetary systems can be balanced against the need for a common regulatory scheme among financial centres to govern the global system has yet to be determined.

8 Conclusions

This book has traced the development of international economic relations primarily through the evolution of international flows of goods, people and capital and through the development of multilateral institutions. Geographically, the story has branched out from the Anglo-American domination of policy-making during and immediately after the war to the growing centrality of the US–European nexus by the 1960s. In the 1970s Japan emerged as a central player due to its phenomenal success in entering the competitive international market for manufactures. This pattern was repeated for other newly industrialising East Asian economies, most prominently by China in the 1990s, so that by the mid-2000s the Sino-American axis became the fulcrum for global economic management. China's success, along with other emerging markets such as Brazil and India, broke open the governance of the international economy in the wake of the demonstrable failure of existing structures after the global financial crisis of 2007.

At the start of the post-war period representatives of forty-four countries came together to agree the Articles of Agreement for the IMF and the World Bank, with their implicit and explicit commitments to freer trade and payments. This broad engagement was the result of a collective understanding that narrow governance of the international system and the emphasis on national over collective interests during the inter-war period had ultimately contributed to the spread and depth of the Great Depression. Very soon after the Bretton Woods meetings, however, economic leadership contracted to the prosperous European and American economies of the 1950s and 1960s as growth was restored. Repeated episodes of systemic crisis in the early 1980s and mid-to-late 1990s prompted reassessments of the global financial architecture, but reforms were slow – reactive rather the pro-active – and ineffective in forestalling further crises. As after the Great Depression, the evident failure of the international system in the global crisis of 2007–8 renewed the justification for a wider engagement, and by 2008 economic governance was widened to the G20. Whether this commitment to broader legitimacy for policy-making will survive the renewal of economic growth remains to be seen.

The story of the post-war years might appear in hindsight to be one of inexorable progress toward a renewed expansion of international economic relations after the Great Reversal of the inter-war period interrupted the late nineteenth century era of globalisation. In fact, however, the liberalisation of trade, capital flows and migration has been shown to be uneven and highly contested. Trade liberalisation was the least controversial; the removal of trade barriers first among Europe and North America and then throughout the developed world led to an era of sustained growth in the 1950s and 1960s, although this success was mainly limited to richer nations of the OECD. Multilateral initiatives were primarily aimed at freeing up trade in manufactured goods, while agricultural producers in rich countries remained highly protected by a range of subsidies and tariffs. The commitment to freer trade at Bretton Woods was replaced by a goal of 'fair' trade in the 1980s as European and American producers faced greater competition first from Japan and then from China. The outcome was a partial return to protectionism on manufactured goods trade through voluntary quotas and export restraints. Despite these limitations, the expansion of international trade since the 1950s has provided opportunities for a range of developed and developing economies to bring their populations out of poverty and raise per capita incomes. Trade was also affected by communication innovations that helped multinational corporations exploit far-flung resources and labour markets to feed growing consumer markets in both developed and developing economies, further adding to integrated markets in goods and services. But the gains from free flows of short-term investment capital appeared less obvious to planners at Bretton Woods with their memory of 'hot money' destabilising the international financial system, and it was not until the 1970s that policy-makers in the developed world embraced the liberalisation of capital markets. The choice of national policy autonomy and stable exchange rates suited the Keynesian economic ideology of the 1950s and 1960s, with its emphasis on government spending, and supported the rise of welfare states in many developed nations. This view was challenged in some developing countries where Prebisch's ideas of structural deficiencies in the global system led to efforts to insulate domestic economies from the competition of international trade in order to diversify away from primary production. By the late 1960s, however, it became more difficult to restrain capital flows due to financial innovation, greater demand for risk-spreading financial products and an erosion of confidence in the pegged exchange rate regime.

Financial innovation helped integrate markets and provided new complex products that appeared to reduce risk in the increasingly volatile environment of the late 1960s and early 1970s. The pegged exchange rates at the core of the system gave way as the dollar was devalued against gold in 1971, sterling floated in June 1972, and the dollar and yen followed in the spring of 1973 in the pursuit of domestic monetary policy sovereignty. European leaders and governments of developing countries continued to value exchange rate stability in some form over policy sovereignty since the costs of exchange rate stability appeared higher. Europe moved toward monetary integration and many developing economies pegged to the US dollar and then to the SDR in the 1970s.

The global financial market attracted praise for helping to redress imbalances both in the 1970s and also the 2000s, channelling savings from surplus to deficit countries, and providing much-needed resources to spread wealth to emerging markets in the decades between. In each case, however, capital flows were ultimately blamed for traumatic financial and economic crises that erupted in each decade. During each round of crisis it became apparent that underlying institutions such as regulation, supervision, transparency and governance were inadequate to ensure well functioning efficient markets. One characteristic of the globalised era has been repeated asset market bubbles that have had greater and greater real impact on economies through integrated financial systems. In the 1980s the Latin American debt crisis revealed market imperfections in flows of information, assessment of sovereign risk, moral hazard and corruption. In the 1990s, the challenges came from both public and private borrowing and government interference in bank lending, as well as the inability to manage the risk of currency mismatch between assets and liabilities. These crises also highlighted the dangers of contagion within groups of emerging markets and their threat to the global banking system.

By the 2000s, financial innovation and excessive risk-taking in the context of asset market bubbles created fragility in the financial systems of the USA and Europe that quickly spread globally through now highly integrated markets. The real impact of this financial implosion was borne through the freezing of trade, unemployment, government bailouts of national banking systems and unprecedented fiscal expenditure to try to sustain employment and investment. These policy reactions drew directly from the lessons of the Great Depression about the danger of allowing the money supply to contract in a banking crisis, and the short-term growth shock appeared to be reversed fairly quickly, although not painlessly in many economies. After all, Ben Bernanke, the Chairman of the Federal Reserve Board in the United States during the crisis, was a scholar of the Great Depression before he took public office.[1] The long-term impact of this recent crisis on regulatory reform, tax burdens on firms and individuals, and ultimately on achieving sustainable growth remains to be seen.

With international capital flows difficult to control and the benefits of freer trade generally agreed, attention has shifted partly to controlling movements of labour to insulate economies from the impact of international economic relations. During the post-war period there was an acceleration of international migration driven by political changes in Europe, the process of European market integration, the spread of labour intensive production in Asia and growing opportunities for skilled employment in many developed economies. However, the fence extended by the United States along the 2,000-mile border with Mexico since 2005, new controls on non-EU immigration into the UK and other European states, and tighter restrictions on visas in response to the perceived threat of terrorism are all expressions of a desire to control the impact of globalisation on national populations, cultures and economies. In the current environment of increased expenditure on social welfare, job insecurity and clashing cultural values, arguments for restricting international migration tend to meet a receptive mood.

As the international economy seems set to enter a new phase with reformed governance structures, renewed importance for the IMF and possible retreat by some states on progress toward free trade and migration, it is wise to reflect on the difficulties and challenges that affected the progress of international economic relations and the huge benefits as well as costs that this process has reaped for the vast majority of the world's population. The scope for extending the benefits of international exchange even more widely in the future is clear, although the history of the post-war decades suggests that this process will likely be highly contested. At the end of its summit in Toronto in June 2010, the G20 pledged its commitment 'to taking concerted actions to sustain the recovery, create jobs and to achieve stronger, more sustainable and more balanced growth' through restoring international trade and strengthening financial institutions. The opening paragraphs of the Articles of Agreement of the IMF in 1944 committed the forty-four member states 'to the promotion and maintenance of high levels of employment and real income and to the development of the productive resources of all members as primary objectives of economic policy'. Arguably we have not travelled that far from the spirit of Bretton Woods despite the transformation of the international economic system.

Glossary

Capital foregoing current consumption in order to generate income over time. Financial capital involves foregoing the use of money now to lend it or invest it in return for interest payments over time and ultimately repayment of the original amount.

Depreciation when the exchange rate or price of a currency declines on the foreign exchange market.

Derivatives financial instruments that are based on the current or future value of a security, bond or other asset, sometimes in combination. They can be traded through an exchange or between individuals (over the counter).

Devaluation when the exchange rate or price of a currency is deliberately reduced, often from one pegged rate to another.

Emigration people moving away from a country with a view to settlement elsewhere.

Exchange rate the price of one currency in terms of another, for example the number of dollars that it costs to buy one pound sterling.

FDI foreign direct investment is an investment across borders where the investor exercises an element of control over the enterprise, such as multinational companies.

Fiscal policy government policy exercised through the government's budget, for example raising/lowering taxes or government spending.

GDP gross domestic product is a measure of the sum total of expenditure on all goods and services produced in an economy. It includes consumption, investment, government spending and exports less imported goods.

Immigration movement of people into a country with a view to settlement.

Inflation the rate at which prices rise in an economy.

Interest the cost of borrowing.

MNC or TNC multinational company or transnational company. A firm that operates in more than one country either through subsidiaries, branches or another form of owning companies in another country.

Monetary policy government policy that aims to affect the money supply in an economy, for example through manipulating interest rates or the amount of lending that banks can engage in.

Per capita a formal expression for 'per person' in the population, sometimes expressed as p.c.

Portfolio investment an investment across borders where the investor does not exercise control over the recipient, for example bonds or shares.

Primary product products that are unprocessed and resource based such as agriculture or mining.

Security/securitisation issuing debt that is linked to assets that are expected to generate income over time. The returns on the security are determined by the returns on the underlying assets.

Tariff a tax on the value of goods imported, usually expressed as a percentage of the value of the product.

Trade balance the total value of exports sold by an economy minus the total value of imported goods from abroad.

Further reading

This book has aimed to provide a general overview of key trends in the development of international economic relations. More extensive treatments are available in a range of recent publications covering different themes.

A useful site to explore the theory and policy of international economics is the International Economics Study Centre (http://internationalecon.com/index.php) begun by Steve Siranovic and supported by Flat World Knowledge.

Global

Clarke, G., *A Farewell to Alms: A Brief Economic History of the World*, Princeton, NJ: Princeton University Press, 2008.

Findlay, R. and O'Rourke, K.H., *Power and Plenty: Trade, War, and the World Economy in the Second Millennium*, Princeton, NJ: Princeton University Press, 2009.

Maddison, A., *Contours of the World Economy 1–2030 AD: Essays in Macro-Economic History*, Oxford: Oxford University Press, 2007.

Reinhart, C.M. and Rogoff, K., *This Time is Different: Eight Centuries of Financial Folly*, Princeton, NJ: Princeton University Press, 2009.

The international monetary system

Eichengreen, B., *Globalizing Capital: A History of the International Monetary System*, 2nd edn, Princeton, NJ: Princeton University Press, 2008.

Obstfeld, M. and Taylor, A.M., *Global Capital Markets: Integration, Crisis, and Growth*, Cambridge: Cambridge University Press, 2004.

Europe

Broadberry, S. and O'Rourke, K.H., eds, *The Cambridge Economic History of Modern Europe Vol. 2: 1870 to the Present*, Cambridge: Cambridge University Press, 2010.

Eichengreen, B., *The European Economy since 1945: Coordinated Capitalism and Beyond*, Princeton, NJ: Princeton University Press, 2008.

Persson, K.G., *An Economic History of Europe*, Cambridge: Cambridge University Press, 2010.

Schultze, M.S., ed., *Western Europe: Economic and Social Change since 1945*, London: Longman, 1999.

China

Bramall, C., *Chinese Economic Development*, London: Routledge, 2009.

Chow, G.C., *China's Economic Transformation*, 2nd edn, Oxford: Blackwell, 2007.

Naughton, B., *The Chinese Economy: Transitions and Growth*, Cambridge, MA: MIT Press, 2007.

Notes

1 Introduction and overview

1 R. Vernon, 'The product cycle hypothesis in a new international environment', *Quarterly Journal of Economics*, 80, 1966, pp. 255–67.
2 An extended application can be found in M. Obstfeld and A. Taylor, *Global Capital Markets: Integration, Crisis, and Growth*, Cambridge: Cambridge University Press, 2004. The original formulation is R.A. Mundell, 'Capital mobility and stabilization policy under fixed and flexible exchange rates', *Canadian Journal of Economic and Political Science*, vol. 29, November 1963.
3 B. Eichengreen, *Golden Fetters: The Gold Standard and the Great Depression, 1919–1939*, Oxford: Oxford University Press, 1992.
4 The UN backdates the break up of the USSR from 1991 to 1990 to allow better comparison by decade.
5 J. Servan-Schreiber, *Le Defi Americain*, Paris: Editions Denoel, 1967. R. Barnet and R. Muller, *Global Reach: The Power of the Multinational Corporations*, New York: Simon & Schuster, 1974. On Japan see D. Halberstam, *The Reckoning*, New York: William Morrow & Co., 1986; and N. Morris, *Japan-Bashing: Anti-Japanism since the 1980s*, London: Routledge, 2010.

2 Rebuilding the international economic system 1945–50

1 There were unsuccessful efforts to co-ordinate exchange rate policy, such as the Tripartite Agreement, the Genoa Conference and the inter-war gold standard, but these failed, partly due to lack of American engagement.
2 J.M. Keynes, *The Economic Consequences of the Peace*, London: Harcourt, Brace & Howe, 1920. J.M. Keynes, *The Economic Consequences of Mr. Churchill*, London: Hogarth Press, 1925.
3 R.N. Gardner, *Sterling Dollar Diplomacy in Current Perspective: The Origins of our International Economic Order*, New York: Columbia University Press, 1980. See also the official histories of the IMF: J.K. Horsefield, *The International Monetary Fund 1945–65: Twenty Years of International Monetary Cooperation Vol. 2 Analysis*, IMF, Washington, 1969; H. James, *International Monetary Cooperation since Bretton Woods*, Oxford: Oxford University Press, 1996.
4 A.S. Milward, *The Reconstruction of Western Europe 1945–51*, London: Methuen, 1984.
5 B. Eichengreen and M. Uzan, 'The Marshall Plan: Economic effects and implications for Eastern Europe and the former Soviet Union', *Economic Policy*, 14, pp. 13–76, 1992.

6 A.S. Milward, *The European Rescue of the Nation-State*, London: Routledge, 1992.
7 Members included all British colonies, Australia, New Zealand, South Africa, Ireland, India, Pakistan, Ceylon (Sri Lanka), Iraq, Persian Gulf states, Kuwait, Egypt, Burma, Libya and Iceland. See C.R. Schenk, *The Decline of Sterling: Managing the Retreat of an International Currency 1945–1992*, Cambridge University Press, 2010.

3 Years of growth 1950–73

1 The G10 included the United States, the UK, West Germany, Italy, Belgium, France, the Netherlands, Canada, Japan and Sweden, who agreed to loan funds to the IMF under the General Arrangements to Borrow in 1962.
2 For a critical review of the contribution of formal integration to European growth, see B. Eichengreen and A. Boltho, 'The economic impact of European integration' in S. Broadberry and K. O'Rourke, eds, *Cambridge Economic History of Modern Europe*, vol. 2, Cambridge: Cambridge University Press, 2010, pp. 268–95.
3 D. Dollar, 'Globalization, poverty and inequality since 1980', *The World Bank Research Observer*, 20, 2005, pp. 145–75.
4 F.C. Deyo, 'Introduction' in F.C. Deyo, ed., *The Political Economy of the New Asian Industrialism*, Ithaca, NY: Cornell University Press, 1987.
5 The Gold Pool included the UK, the USA, Germany, Italy, France, Belgium, the Netherlands and Switzerland.

4 Years of crisis 1973–85

1 J.D. Sachs and A.M. Warner, 'The curse of natural resources', *European Economic Review*, 45(4–6), 2001, pp. 827–38. H. Mehlum, K. Moene, R. Torvik, 'Institutions and the resource curse', *Economic Journal*, 116(508), 2006, pp. 1–20.
2 A.H. Amsden, *Asia's Next Giant: South Korea and Late Industrialization*, Oxford: Oxford University Press, p. 95.
3 A. Schwartz, 'International Debt; what's fact and what's fiction?', *Economic Inquiry*, 27, 1989, pp. 1–19.
4 See the IMF official history of this period, J. Boughton, *Silent Revolution: The IMF 1979–89*, IMF, Washington, 2001, p. 428. Available online at www.imf. org/external/pubs/ft/history/2001/index.htm.
5 Bank of England, *Quarterly Bulletin*, 17(3), 1977.

5 The start of the second globalisation 1985–95

1 For a review, see J. Scholte, *Globalization: A Critical Introduction,* London: Palgrave Macmillan, 2000; J.E. Stiglitz, *Globalization and its Discontents*, New York: W.W. Norton, 2002.
2 This term was coined by John Williamson in 1989 to identify ten policies that many in Washington agreed should be applied in Latin America.
3 UNCTAD, *Development and Globalization: Facts and Figures*, 2004.
4 See the discussion in R. Findlay and K. O'Rourke, *Power and Plenty: Trade, War and the World Economy in the Second Millennium*, Princeton, NJ: Princeton University Press, 2007.

5   UN, *World Economic and Social Survey*, 2004.
6   Department of Immigration and Multicultural Affairs, Australia.
7   UN, *World Economic and Social Survey*, 2004, p. 38. Of an estimated 7 million irregular migrants in January 2000, 4.8 million were likely from Mexico.
8   Richer territories in this estimate were Australia, Europe, Japan, New Zealand and Northern America. Poorer territories included African nations, Asian nations (excluding Japan), Latin America and the Caribbean, Melanesia, Micronesia and Polynesia.
9   OECD, *Economic Outlook*, 71, 2002.
10   Sceptical views of the relationship between openness to trade and income growth include J.A. Frankel and D. Romer, 'Does trade cause growth?' *American Economic Review*, 89(3), pp. 379–99; and R. Rodriguez and D. Rodrik, 'Trade policy and economic growth: a skeptic's guide to the cross-national evidence', *NBER Macroeconomics Annual*, 15, 2000, pp. 261–325.
11   UNCTAD, *Development and Globalization: Facts and Figures*, 2008.
12   For a review, see P.B. Henry, 'Capital account liberalization: theory, evidence and speculation', *Journal of Economic Literature*, 45(4), 2007, pp. 887–935.
13   E. Apel, *European Monetary Integration 1950–2002*, London: Routledge, 1998.

6   The acceleration of globalisation and renewed crises 1995–9

1   In 2004 the countries that joined the EU were: the Czech Republic, Estonia, Cyprus, Latvia, Lithuania, Hungary, Malta, Poland, Slovakia and Slovenia.
2   P. Lamy, 'Director-General's remarks at the informal TNC', WTO, Geneva, 16 November 2006. Available at www.wto.org/english/news_e/news06_e/tnc_dg_stat_16nov06_e.htm.
3   For a brief overview, see L. Hudson Teslik, 'Nafta's Economic Impact', *US Council on Foreign Relations*, 2009. Available at www.cfr.org/publication/15790/naftas_economic_impact.html.
4   B. Eichengreen, *Towards a New International Financial Architecture: A Practical Post-Asia Agenda*, Washington, DC: Institute for International Economics, 1999; P.B. Kenen, *The International Financial Architecture: What's New, What's Missing*, Washington, DC: Peterson Institute, 2001.
5   J.A. Whitt, Jr., 'The Peso Crisis', *Federal Reserve Bank of Atlanta Economic Review*, January/February 1996. G.O. Martinez, 'What lessons does the Mexican crisis hold for recovery in Asia', *Finance and Development*, 35(2), June 1998.
6   J. Sachs, A. Tornell and A. Valasco, 'The Mexican peso crisis: sudden death or death foretold?' *Journal of International Economics*, 41, 1996, pp. 265–83.
7   A. Krueger and A. Tornell, *The Role of Bank Restructuring in Recovering from Crises: Mexico, 1995–1998*, UCLA mimeo, 1999.
8   A. Chopra *et al.*, *From Crisis to Recovery in South Korea: Strategy, Achievements and Lessons*, IMF Working Paper, 2001. Available at www.imf.org/external/pubs/ft/wp/2001/wp01154.pdf.
9   Policy Development and Review Department, *Lessons from the Crisis in Argentina*, IMF, 2003. Available at www.imf.org/external/np/pdr/lessons/100803.pdf.

7 Lessons not learned

1 Examples of such concerns include Al Gore and Davis Guggenheim's Oscar-winning film *An Inconvenient Truth*, 2006; N. Stern, *The Economics of Climate Change: The Stern Review*, Cambridge: Cambridge University Press, 2007; R. Layard, *Happiness: Lessons from a new science*, London: Penguin, 2006; A. Offer, *The Challenge of Affluence: Self-control and Well-being in the USA and Britain since 1950*, Oxford: Oxford University Press, 2007.
2 R. Barrell, J. FitzGerald and R. Riley, 'EU enlargement and migration: assessing the macroeconomic impacts', National Institute of Economic and Social Research Discussion Paper No. 292, March 2007.
3 Eurostat, 'Remittance flows to and from the EU', 2007. Available at http://epp.eurostat.ec.europa.eu/cache/ITY_OFFPUB/KS-RA-07-025/EN/KS-RA-07-025-EN.PDF.
4 J. O'Neill, 'Building better global economic BRICs', *Global Economics Papers*, 66, November 2001. Available at www2.goldmansachs.com/ideas/brics/building-better-doc.pdf.
5 US Bureau of Economic Affairs. Available at www.bea.gov/newsreleases/international/trade/trad_time_series.xls.
6 The IMF data on currency distribution of reserves covers about 60 per cent of total global reserves (see IMF Currency Composition of Official Foreign Exchange Reserves at www.imf.org/external/np/sta/cofer/eng/index.htm).
7 Zhou Xiaochuan, speech, 'Reform the international monetary system', 23 March 2009. Available at www.pbc.gov.cn/english/detail.asp?col=6500&id=178. J. Stiglitz, *Making Globalization Work*, New York: W.W. Norton, 2006.
8 The risk rating for AAA to AA– sovereign and corporate claims was 20 per cent; for A+ to A– sovereign and corporate claims was 50 per cent. The risk rating for residential mortgages was 35 per cent. There was a caveat that this assumed 'the existence of substantial margin of additional security over the amount of the loan based on strict valuation rules' (Basel Committee on Banking Supervision, *Basel II: International Convergence of Capital Measurement and Capital Standards: A Revised Framework – Comprehensive Version*, 'Part 2: The First Pillar – Minimum Capital Requirements', 2006. Available at www.bis.org/publ/bcbs128.htm).
9 Total emigration was 10,612 including non-Icelandic residents, many of whom were Poles returning home.
10 A useful overview is available in R. Baldwin, *The Great Trade Collapse: What Caused it and What Does it Mean?*. Available at www.voxeu.org.
11 The G7 countries are France, Italy, Germany, the USA, Japan, Canada and the UK. The G20 members are Argentina, Australia, Brazil, Canada, China, EU, France, Germany, India, Indonesia, Italy, Japan, Mexico, Russia, Saudi Arabia, South Africa, Republic of Korea, Turkey, the UK and the USA.
12 The FSB grew out of the Financial Stability Forum established in 1999 with a smaller membership.

8 Conclusions

1 B.S. Bernanke, *Essays on the Great Depression*, Princeton, NJ: Princeton University Press, 2004.

Index

The Ideal Companion to
International Economic Relations Since 1945

Doing History

Mark Donnelly, and **Claire Norton**, both St. Mary's University College, UK

'**I thought the book was really excellent, probably being the best of its kind I have read**' – *Alun Munslow, University of Chichester, UK*

Aimed at students beginning degrees, this is the ideal introduction to studying history as an academic subject at university. *Doing History* presents the ideas and debates that shape how we "do" history today, covering arguments about nature of historical knowledge and the function of historical writing, whether we can really ever know what happened in the past, what sources historians depend on, and whether the historians' version of history has more value than popular histories.

This practical and accessible introduction to the discipline introduces students to these key discussions, familiarises them with the important terms and issues, equips them with the necessary vocabulary and encourages them to think about, and engage with, these questions. Clearly structured and accessibly written, it is an essential volume for all students embarking on the study of history.

2011: 198x129: 224pp
Pb: 978-0-415-56577-6

For more information and to order a copy visit
www.routledge.com/9780415565776

Available from all good bookshops